WOMEN HEROES OF THE US ARMY

OTHER BOOKS IN THE WOMEN OF ACTION SERIES

Bold Women of Medicine by Susan M. Latta

Code Name Pauline by Pearl Witherington Cornioley, edited by Kathryn J. Atwood

Courageous Women of the Civil War by M. R. Cordell

Courageous Women of the Vietnam War by Kathryn J. Atwood

Double Victory by Cheryl Mullenbach

The Many Faces of Josephine Baker by Peggy Caravantes

Marooned in the Arctic by Peggy Caravantes

Reporting Under Fire by Kerrie L. Hollihan

Seized by the Sun by James W. Ure

She Takes a Stand by Michael Elsohn Ross

This Noble Woman by Michael Greenburg

Women Aviators by Karen Bush Gibson

Women Heroes of the American Revolution by Susan Casey

Women Heroes of World War I by Kathryn J. Atwood

Women Heroes of World War II by Kathryn J. Atwood

Women Heroes of World War II—the Pacific Theater by Kathryn J. Atwood

Women in Blue by Cheryl Mullenbach

Women in Space by Karen Bush Gibson

Women of Colonial America by Brandon Marie Miller

Women of Steel and Stone by Anna M. Lewis

Women of the Frontier by Brandon Marie Miller

A World of Her Own by Michael Elsohn Ross

WOMEN HEROES
OF THE US ARMY

★ ★ ★ ★ ★ ★ ★ ★ ★ ★ ★ ★

Remarkable Soldiers from the American Revolution to Today

ANN McCALLUM STAATS

CHICAGO
REVIEW
PRESS

Published by Chicago Review Press Incorporated
814 North Franklin Street
Chicago, Illinois 60610
ISBN 978-0-914091-24-0

Library of Congress Cataloging-in-Publication Data
Names: McCallum, Ann, 1965– author.
Title: Women heroes of the US Army : remarkable soldiers from the American
   Revolution to today / Ann McCallum Staats.
Other titles: Women heroes of the U.S. Army
Description: First edition. | Chicago, Illinois : Chicago Review Press
   Incorporated, [2019] | Audience: Ages: 12+ | Includes bibliographical
   references and index.
Identifiers: LCCN 2018053583 (print) | LCCN 2019000664 (ebook) | ISBN
   9780914091431 (adobe pdf) | ISBN 9780914091479 (kindle) | ISBN
   9780914091585 (epub) | ISBN 9780914091240 (cloth)
Subjects: LCSH: Women soldiers—United States—Biography—Juvenile
   literature. | Women soldiers—United States—History—Juvenile literature.
   | Women and the military—United States—History—Juvenile literature. |
   United States. Army—Biography—Juvenile literature. | United States.
   Army—History—Juvenile literature. | United States—History,
   Military—Juvenile literature.
Classification: LCC UB418.W65 (ebook) | LCC UB418.W65 M37 2019 (print) | DDC
   355.0092/520973—dc23
LC record available at https://lccn.loc.gov/2018053583

Interior design: Sarah Olson

Printed in the United States of America
5 4 3 2 1

CONTENTS

Introduction. vii

Time Line of Major US Military Operations. xiii

**Part I Early America: The American Revolution
and the Civil War** 1

Margaret Cochran Corbin: Ready, Aim! 5

Sarah Rosetta Wakeman: A Private Volunteer 16

Cathay Williams: Buffalo Woman. 26

**Part II The World at War: World War I
and World War II**. 39

Grace Banker: Number, Please. 44

Oveta Culp Hobby: The Little Colonel 58

Charity Adams Earley: Letters from Home. 72

Margaret KC Yang: Pearl of Oʻahu 87

Part III Global Conflict: The Late 20th Century 99

Elizabeth P. Hoisington: Good Old Army. 103

Celia Adolphi: Farm Girl to Major General 115

LeAnn Swieczkowski: Petite and Powerful 126

Part IV Current Conflicts: War in Modern Times 141

Mary Hostetler: Citizen Soldier—Rock Steady 144

Stephanie Lincoln: Pretty Good
at This Army Thing 158

Leigh Ann Hester: Silver Performer 168

Deborah Kotulich: On the Shoulders of Giants 179

Acknowledgments 191

Glossary 193

Notes 197

Bibliography 207

Index 213

INTRODUCTION

"There will be no exceptions."

On December 3, 2015, the Pentagon Press Briefing Room was packed. Secretary of Defense Ash Carter stood at the podium and looked over the crowd. ". . . those who serve," he said, "are not judged based on who they are or where they come from, but rather what they have to offer to help defend this country."

He was talking about the final obstacle for women serving in the US military. Starting on New Year's Day 2016, everyone who qualified and met the standard—male *or* female—could now legally serve in any position and in any branch of the military. For the first time in history, the US military eliminated all gender-based restrictions. Carter explained what this meant. "They'll be allowed to drive tanks, fire mortars, and lead infantry soldiers into combat. They'll be able to serve as Army Rangers and Green Berets, Navy SEALs, Marine Corps infantry, Air Force parajumpers, and everything else that was previously open to men."

The thing was, though, women were *already* serving in vital, sometimes dangerous roles. They had led men into combat, been captured by the enemy, and fired heavy weapons during life or death firefights. Since earliest times, women had been wounded, even killed, in battle. Throughout history, one woman after another had demonstrated selfless acts of incredible courage, a tenacious resolve that helped win conflicts everywhere. Yet the process of full integration happened gradually as the debate over women's roles in the military simmered for centuries.

The birth of the nation was marked by war. In 1775, as colonial America battled Great Britain for independence, some felt that a woman's place was far from the combat zone and away from the horrors of war. Despite this attitude, hundreds of women followed husbands, brothers, and lovers to battle. They marched behind the troops as camp followers, supporting the soldiers by cooking, doing laundry and other essential tasks, and tending to the wounded. Some, like Margaret Cochran Corbin, served directly on the battlefield. In the midst of the fighting, she carried pitchers of water to the soldiers, helping to create the legend of "Molly Pitcher." When her husband was killed as he stood firing a cannon, she stepped in and fired shot after shot until she was too grievously injured to continue. Later earning a military pension, Margaret was one of America's earliest female soldiers.

Despite this direct involvement, it was still illegal—and shocking—for women to participate in actual combat. During the US Civil War, an estimated hundreds of women did anyway. By the mid-1800s the country was deeply divided, and the rift only got worse. When war erupted in 1861, patriotic zeal—on both sides—reached a fever pitch. Women from both the North and the South refused to stand on the sidelines. Historians estimate that 400 or more women cut their hair short, changed their names, and disguised themselves as men in order to enlist. Sometimes their gender was quickly discovered and commanders tossed them out immediately. In other instances, female soldiers served for years, never letting on that they were not men. Case after case documents the valor and fortitude of these women.

Another instance of women at war was during World War I when thousands of nurses deployed overseas and on the home front to care for wounded soldiers. In addition, the American Expeditionary Force (AEF) under General John Pershing desperately needed experts to operate the newly invented telephone switchboards they had installed to communicate with troops. The War Department recruited American women to solve this problem. Soon, over 200 "Hello Girls" sailed to France, many taking up positions perilously close to the front lines of the fighting. Despite their patriotism—and the danger they encountered—the army initially denied these women veteran status when they returned home to the United States, dubbing them "civilian contractors." It took decades to rectify this issue.

The dispute over women's place in war remained quietly in the background until the next major conflict. The United States was a hair's breadth from entering World War II when the idea for a Women's Army Auxiliary Corps (WAAC) took root. The plan was for WAACs to take over noncombatant jobs from men. They would therefore "free a man to fight." The WAAC's first director was Oveta Culp Hobby, the first and only woman awarded full colonel status. She spoke to the first class of officer candidates in 1942: "You have given up comfortable homes. Highly paid positions. Leisure. You have taken off silk and put on khaki. And all for essentially the same reason—you have a debt and a date. A debt to democracy, a date with destiny."

Recruitment for the WAAC swelled as thousands of women competed to get in. But the organization itself was cumbersome. Since it was an auxiliary and not an integral component of the army, there were constant logistical problems about where to procure supplies or who to go to for help. In 1943 the War Department dropped the auxiliary status and the WAAC became the Women's Army Corps (WAC), a recognized branch of the Regular Army. However, rank advancement was capped at lieutenant colonel (except for the director) and women still trained separately from men. Female officers commanded other women. By the end of the war, over 150,000 women had served in the WAC.

With victory in Europe and then in the Pacific theater, many felt there was no longer a need for female soldiers. However, in 1948, President Harry S. Truman signed into law the Women's Armed Services Integration Act, ensuring that women were a permanent fixture in all branches of the military. Although with far fewer members—the law included a 2 percent cap on the number of women allowed to serve—WACs went on to greater and greater responsibility and tackled military challenges never before accomplished by a woman. In 1967 there was another major step forward when two limitations for women were removed: the recruitment cap and rank restrictions. Soon, two women, Anna Mae Hays and Elizabeth P. Hoisington, were promoted to brigadier generals, the first females to achieve this rank. Others followed, including Celia Adolphi, who was the first woman promoted to two-star general—major general—in the US Army Reserve. In 2008 Ann Dunwoody was the first female to attain the highest peacetime active-duty rank, that of four-star general.

Little by little, the structure of the army changed to reflect modern times. For the first time, the US Military Academy opened its doors to women in 1976. Of the 119 initial female cadets, 62 met the same grueling standards as men and graduated four years later. Next, Congress disestablished the WAC on

October 20, 1978, while keeping some jobs still closed to women. Officially, females were excluded from careers that involved direct combat. Unofficially, the lines were much more blurred. During the invasion of Panama in 1989, Captain Linda Bray led her team into a three-hour firefight that left three people dead. Next, enemy forces took female prisoners early in the War on Terror. Then, women like Leigh Ann Hester earned medals for their actions in combat—Hester was the first female Silver Star recipient for valor in combat. Clearly, women were showing a fierce and resilient ability to face difficult challenges, to excel in the heat of incredible hardship, and to earn the esteem of their fellow soldiers.

Eleanor Roosevelt, champion of women in the army, once stated, "Courage is more exhilarating than fear and in the long run it is easier. We do not have to become heroes overnight. Just a step at a time, meeting each thing that comes up, seeing it is not as dreadful as it appeared, discovering we have the strength to stare it down."

Today both male and female soldiers live the slogan "Army Strong." They work, fight, and serve—together.

TIME LINE OF MAJOR
US MILITARY OPERATIONS

1775–1783	American Revolution
1812–1815	War of 1812
1846–1848	Mexican-American War
1861–1865	Civil War
1898–1899	Spanish-American War
1917–1918	World War I
1941–1945	World War II
1950–1953	Korean War
1955–1975	Vietnam War
1990–1991	Gulf War: "Operation Desert Storm"
1992–1995	Somali Civil War: "Operation Restore Hope"
1993–1995	Bosnian War: "Operation Deny Flight"
2001–2017	War in Afghanistan: "Operation Enduring Freedom"
2003–2011	War in Iraq: "Operation Iraqi Freedom," "Operation New Dawn"
2014–present	War on ISIS: "Operation Inherent Resolve"

PART I

Early America

The American Revolution and the Civil War

★ ★ ★ ★ ★

War marked the birth of the United States. America's Revolutionary War, a struggle for independence against the superior forces of the British Army, took place from 1775 to 1783. Men marched, discharged cannons, fired guns, and skirmished in close combat to forge an infant nation. However, men were not the only beneficiaries of this bold, new endeavor. Women were just as invested in the war's outcome—their lives were also at stake.

Battle after battle erupted throughout the land as women followed husbands, brothers, and loved ones into war. Sometimes they stayed on the sidelines, managing critical tasks like caring for the wounded or providing food for famished soldiers. In other cases, like that of Margaret Cochran Corbin, women were in the thick of the fight, doing what needed to be done.

In America's early history, most people lived on farms and in small towns. At the time, there were separate expectations for men and women. Things like cooking, cleaning, washing, and sewing were considered women's work. The "weaker sex" was not to be involved in matters of politics or war. It was surprising then—shocking for the times—when women proved that they, too, could make very fine soldiers.

During the US Civil War, which lasted from 1861 to 1865, it was still illegal for women to enlist as soldiers, yet hundreds did anyway. They disguised themselves in men's clothing and joined the ranks of both the Union and Confederate armies to fight in bloody battles. There were many reasons for doing so. Some wanted to be near a loved one. Some wanted the better opportunities afforded a man. The army offered a secure job and steady paycheck, much more money than most women could hope to earn anywhere else. Many other women joined for patriotic reasons. On August 26, 1864, the New York Times newspaper ran a story about two women who had imperson- ated men in order to serve in the Union army: "Their enlist- ment was prompted by patriotic motives only; they wanted to do a small share towards 'licking the rebs [Confederate army soldiers].'" As scandalous as it was, women risked discovery and social humiliation to serve their country.

Whatever their reason for doing so, women had to over- come many obstacles to enlist. Loreta Velazquez, an author at the time, was very interested in soldiering, and went to great lengths to describe how a woman could fool others into think- ing she was a man. The obvious problem, Loreta pointed out, was that a woman's body did not look like a man's. "A woman's waist, as a general thing, is tapering, and her hips very large in comparison with those of a man." In order to disguise her feminine form, a woman needed to dress in men's clothing, the bulkier the better. For someone who had always worn a skirt— it was a social taboo not to—men's breeches were difficult to get used to. In addition, any female who wanted to become a soldier had to not only cut her hair short but also learn to move and sound like a man. One slipup meant she would be tossed out of the army and possibly even sent to jail.

Women did have one advantage: with so many young boys joining the ranks, the beardless face and smooth complexion of a soldier did not usually create suspicion. With enough confidence and luck, it was possible, then, to disguise oneself as a man. But there was another, more challenging hurdle: all potential recruits had to pass a mandatory medical inspection.

A surgeon had to sign off that every new enlistee was fit to serve, both mentally and physically. Of course, any recruit suspected of being a woman did not qualify. Luckily, a medical examination during this time was less than thorough. Desperate for "men" to serve, the surgeon might check the recruit's teeth (which were needed to tear open a bullet cartridge) and trigger finger. Given the modesty of the day for females *and* males, undressing was not part of the examination. As long as a woman did not give herself away—one documented case describes a woman inadvertently curtseying instead of bowing—she could pass the test and sign on as a soldier. Some females' disguises were so successful they served for years. In 1865 the *St. Paul Pioneer* stated, "A married woman named Clayton has been passed to her home in Minnesota, having enlisted two years."

Cathay Williams was one of the long-serving soldiers. A former slave, she was freed when Union soldiers swept through her community in Jefferson City, Missouri. She enlisted at the close of the Civil War and served for over two years without anyone discovering that "he" was a "she."

Another example is the soldier buried as Private Lyons Wakeman at Chalmette National Cemetery in New Orleans. If not for letters home that her family preserved for generations and finally shared, the world would never have realized this private was a woman, Sarah Rosetta Wakeman.

Because of the necessary deception, historians may never know the exact number of women who fought in the United States' early conflicts, though estimates range in the hundreds. Regardless of number, the documented cases we do have show brave and audacious women who were not afraid to defy convention to take up arms in defense of the nation.

Margaret Cochran Corbin

Ready, Aim!

The grave was located in section 11, row A, at the West Point Cemetery in Orange County, New York. On October 21, 2016, workers building a new retaining wall accidentally disturbed the burial site, exposing human remains. A forensics team was called in. Careful analysis determined that the remains were not from the person listed on the nearby monument. The grave was supposed to be that of Margaret Cochran Corbin, a Revolutionary War hero and one of only two women to receive a soldier's pension during the American Revolution. Instead, modern science confirmed that the skeletal remains were from a tall, muscular man.

This news was particularly disappointing to members of the Daughters of the American Revolution (DAR), an organization founded in 1890. With membership limited to women directly descended from patriots of the American Revolution, one mission of the society is to safeguard history. Nearly 100 years ago, on March 16, 1926, members of the local chapter of the DAR were involved in a significant historical undertaking. Spurred on by hazy rumors and tantalizing clues from various documents, they were looking for the gravesite of a fellow member. The "fellow" they were searching for was patriot Margaret Corbin.

For months the group had been scouring the lands of the wealthy financier J. P. Morgan located near the West Point campus. They were looking for a specific cedar tree that locals remembered had been planted at the head of Margaret Corbin's grave. Then the grandson of an old riverboat captain involved in Margaret's burial pointed to an old gravesite—there was a cedar tree stump at its head—and the DAR members felt sure that they had found the remains of "Captain Molly." A surgeon at the West Point hospital confirmed their conclusion. He attested that the skeletal remains were female and that the damaged bones were consistent with wounds Margaret had received in life. Further proof was that, of the few teeth remaining, the ones on the right were worn down as if from constantly clamping down on a clay pipe. Margaret was known to have done just that.

With great excitement, the DAR carefully collected the remains and placed them in a flag-draped coffin. At a reinterment ceremony shortly afterward, the coffin was lowered into in a hallowed spot in the West Point Cemetery with full military honors. A monument to the legendary Margaret Cochran Corbin was erected nearby.

But why all this fuss over a grave?

Who was Margaret Cochran Corbin and why did she deserve such special treatment?

She was:

An orphan and a soldier's wife.

A camp follower, performing sometimes mundane but essential tasks, such as cleaning and cooking for the marching

Commemorative coin.
*Daughters of the American
Revolution Medal:
Margaret Cochran Corbin,
Revolutionary War*

soldiers of America's
Revolutionary War.

A heroine in the
American Revolution and
the first woman to receive
a military pension from the US
government in recognition of her bravery.

Margaret earned her place in history approximately 150 years
before the DAR members went looking for her grave. Many
facts about her life and accomplishments have grown hazy over
time. No doubt, some stories about Margaret have been exag-
gerated and embellished. However, some facts *are* known, like
when she lost her parents.

Margaret Cochran was born in Franklin County, Pennsylvania, on November 12, 1751. A short time later, tragedy struck.
In June 1756, the year Margaret turned five, she and her brother
were staying at an uncle's nearby farm. Before this time, little
Margaret hadn't paid much attention to the French and Indian
War. Of course, she had heard adults talking about the fierce
fight raging between Britain and France as they battled for pos-
session of North American lands. She knew, too, that the original inhabitants, the Native Americans, had been drawn into the
conflict and many were fighting on the side of the French. So far
these problems had not really affected life on her family's farm.
However, that was about to change.

CAMP FOLLOWERS

The Revolutionary War lasted from 1775 to 1783. The conflict started when American patriots attempted to break ties with powerful Britain. Ultimately, the colonists won the war and the United States became an independent country. However, this was in spite of George Washington's inferior army, which was ragged, ill fed, and often outnumbered. While the British had impressive red uniforms, many patriots were lucky to be wearing shoes. And food was sporadic at best. Still, though supplies were tight and conditions were tough, Washington's army could count on one thing: the help of camp followers. Historians claim that America could not have won this war without the participation of these hardy women who supported the soldiers by gathering food, cooking, laundering clothes, nursing the wounded, and performing other vital tasks. George Washington often lamented the motley group of female followers, but even he knew they were necessary to support the day-to-day life of America's soldiers.

Anticipating trouble, a resident of the region, Samuel Bigham, had built a blockhouse and small stockade a couple of years before. The wooden building could provide defense to traders and settlers and included holes from which to fire guns in multiple directions. Despite this protection, a Native American raid resulted in many deaths. Margaret's father was one of those killed and scalped during the Fort Bigham Massacre. Her mother's body was not among the dead, but Margaret never

Margaret Corbin, watercolor on paper by Herbert Knoetel, c.1955. *West Point Museum Collection, United States Military Academy*

saw her again. Overnight, Margaret and her brother became orphans. If not for their uncle taking them in, they would have had nowhere to go.

Life in their new home was hard. Margaret worked long days on her uncle's farm, growing into a strong young woman and a valuable worker. In 1772 she married another farmer, a man named John Corbin. Life soon took another turn. Margaret's husband joined the First Company of the Pennsylvania Artillery in 1775. Colonists from all over America were fighting for independence from Britain in the conflict known as the American Revolution.

When John packed up and left his farm, Margaret was not about to stay behind. She followed John and the rest of the army and helped with important duties like cooking, laundering, and caring for the wounded—even bringing water to the men on the battlefield. Margaret pitched in wherever she could help, allowing the men to focus on being soldiers.

Except one day Margaret became a soldier too.

Margaret marched for months with the Continental Army. Her husband, John, was a matross—a cannoneer. His job was to work with the gunner to fire one of the field cannons. While he learned the proper procedure for firing the artillery, Margaret watched and learned beside him.

Attention!

Search piece, tend vent, advance sponge, handle cartridge, ram down cartridge, put in wadding, put in shot, prime, take aim . . . FIRE!

Margaret took careful note as the men followed a step-by-step process to fire the cannon. One man checked the barrel for debris from the previous shot using a special rod and hook. Another closed the vent on top to prevent air from igniting any residual powder. The men swabbed the inside of the barrel with a damp sponge. They took a cartridge from the ammunition chest and carefully rammed it inside the barrel, followed by some wadding and the shot. A quill was placed into the vent for a fuse. Finally, the gunner took aim and brought the linstock—a long pole to hold the burning match—close enough to light the quill.

BOOM!

The noise was deafening and the smoke dense, but that did not deter Margaret. She stood by in the thick of things, bringing water and paying attention as the men repeated the process. They took cartridge after cartridge from the ammunition chest and fired at the advancing enemy. They were shooting grapeshot, small metal balls that spread across the battlefield and caused incredible damage.

November 6, 1776, was cold and there was a light snow. John Corbin's orders were to set up the cannon and help defend a nearby ridge. Margaret was right there next to her husband among the flying bullets. As the Redcoats, Hessians (German mercenaries), and even some kilted Highlanders attacked, Margaret worked nonstop bringing water to the gun crew.

Suddenly, it happened. A bullet found the cannon's gunner and killed him. Then John was hit too. He died instantly.

((★))

ATTACK ON FORT WASHINGTON, 1776

Located strategically next to the Hudson River, Fort Washington—with Fort Lee on the opposite shore—was an important American stronghold. The idea was to stop British warships from sailing farther up the river. In addition to the forts, patriots had riddled the water with obstacles to try to prevent enemy ships from getting past. With all these fortifications, it would be tough for the British to launch a successful attack. At least, that is what the commander at Fort Washington thought. Despite relatively few troops and a poorly designed fort, Colonel Robert Magaw was certain the garrison could hold out until at least December of that year. British lieutenant general William Howe decided to prove him wrong.

When the British attacked, they had a force of over 8,000 men, including a contingent of Hessians—German mercenaries. There were about 3,000 patriot troops to defend Fort Washington.

((★))

Margaret barely paused before stepping into her late husband's role. She knew how to fire the cannon—and she knew someone had to take over. Margaret fired shot after shot. She didn't stop until she, too, was seriously injured. Grapeshot tore through her shoulder, chest, and jaw. Desperately wounded but not dead, she slumped to the ground, unable to continue.

Meanwhile, the enemy kept coming. Victory was just a matter of time, so the British commander sent a messenger forward. He gave Colonel Robert Magaw one choice: surrender.

Margaret found out the details of the battle later. She learned that, outnumbered and with no hope for victory, the Continental Army surrendered. She learned that 59 Americans perished, though 84 enemy soldiers were also killed. She was one of 96 Continental soldiers wounded in the battle.

The hours and days after the battle were difficult for Margaret. As soon as the fighting ended, she was taken prisoner but

AMERICA REVOLTS!

The French and Indian War ended just over 20 years before the American Revolution began. After that earlier conflict, Britain claimed most of the land in North America. However, the war had been expensive. How would Britain recoup all the money it had spent on soldiers, equipment, and supplies? British Parliament decided to tax the colonists in America. After all, the colonists were the ones who benefitted from the war, right?

Some colonists—the Loyalists—were willing to pay extra taxes. Others, called Patriots, said it was unfair for Britain to collect taxes and create colonial laws when Americans themselves had no say in the British government. The talk in both countries heated up. Finally, things came to a boil, and on July 4, 1776, America adopted the Declaration of Independence. This document stated that Britain was no longer in charge. The United States was now a separate country and would set up its own laws and government. Britain had one thing to say: war! American colonists fought against the British in the conflict known as the American Revolution.

Molly Pitcher. *George Alfred Williams*

then paroled with the other wounded prisoners. First they were ferried across the river to Fort Lee. From there she traveled in a straw-filled wagon to Philadelphia. All the jolting way to the hospital, she somehow stayed alive. Finally, after a period of rest and only partial recovery—she never did regain full use of her left arm—Margaret became a member of the army's otherwise all-male Invalid Regiment at West Point, New York. She put an old artillery jacket over her petticoat and gave herself a new name: Captain Molly.

Captain Molly's health continued to decline. By the time she mustered out of the Invalid Corps in 1783, she needed serious help. Before this, on June 29, 1779, the state of Pennsylvania had awarded her a one-time sum of $30 to "relieve her present necessities." Further, the council ordered "that the case of Margaret Corbin, who was wounded and utterly disabled at Fort Washington, while she heroically filled the post of her husband, who was killed by her side serving a piece of Artillery, be recommended to a further consideration of the Board of War." On July 6, the Continental Congress assigned her a pension equivalent to half the sum given to a male private. It was a landmark decision. After all, she was the first woman ever awarded a US military pension and, therefore, the first woman recognized as a soldier of the US Army.

Along with the pension, Captain Molly was due a measure of rum. The officer in charge expressed his misgivings: "Perhaps it would not be prudent to give them [her rations] to her all in liquor." She was known to be loud and rude, and the officer felt that Molly would drink to excess and become unruly. The citizens in town were already aware of her quick temper and unladylike behavior. Not only did she smoke a clay pipe—unacceptable for women, according to the norms of the day—but she was so disagreeable that the other ladies in town canceled a monument they had been planning to erect for her.

Molly did eventually get several monuments, but not while she was alive. For the last years of her life, she lived in Buttermilk Falls (later renamed Highland Falls) and women in town took turns caring for her. The government paid for her food and lodging, but it was barely enough to survive. Money was so scarce that she had some of her clothes made from old bedsheets. Captain Molly died just before her 50th birthday and was buried with little fanfare. Now, the memorial located in the West Point Cemetery reads, IN APPRECIATION OF HER DEEDS FOR THE CAUSE OF LIBERTY AND THAT HER HEROISM MAY NOT BE FORGOTTEN.

★ LEARN MORE ★

Heroines of the American Revolution: America's Founding Mothers by Diane Silcox-Jarrett, illustrated by Art Seiden (Chapel Hill, NC: Green Angel, 1998)

Women Heroes of the American Revolution: 20 Stories of Espionage, Sabotage, Defiance, and Rescue by Susan Casey (Chicago: Chicago Review Press, 2017)

Sarah Rosetta Wakeman

A Private Volunteer

"Have you a husband in the regiment?" I questioned.

"No."

"A lover or friend?"

"No, I didn't know any of them."

"Well, why did you enlist?"

"I thought I'd like camp life, and I did."

Annie Wittenmyer, a social reformer during the 1800s, wrote this excerpt in her memoir. She was reflecting on an encounter she had with an unknown female soldier during the American Civil War. The woman, fighting on the side of the Union army, had been wounded—a nasty, deep gash in her thigh—and lay on the battlefield until taken prisoner by the Confederate army. Since she had short, cropped hair and was wearing men's clothing, no one suspected that "he" was a "she" until a doctor tended to her injury. The woman was hustled back to the Union lines, where her commanding officer indignantly and promptly discharged her. Women did *not* fight in men's battles. Women were certainly *not* soldiers.

Except that they were.

Like this woman, Sarah Rosetta Wakeman—she went by Rosetta—decided to risk discovery and enlist as a soldier in the US Army. She knew it was illegal to do so as a woman, and she knew she could be thrown in prison if ever her secret was made known. Despite the danger, Rosetta decided that soldiering was exactly what she was going to do.

Rosetta grew up on a dairy farm in Chenango County, New York. Born on January 16, 1843, she was the oldest of nine

》》》》》》》》》》》》》》》 ★ 《《《《《《《《《《《《《《《

WOMEN IN THE CIVIL WAR

Men fought in the American Civil War from April 12, 1861, to May 9, 1865. Like Rosetta, many women disguised themselves as men in order to fight in the war too. At the time, it was against the law for women to become soldiers. Not only that, but there was a clearly marked line between acceptable behavior for men and for women. All women were to wear full dresses that covered them from ankles to neck. They were to always behave in a ladylike manner.

Despite this, historians estimate that hundreds of women enlisted, though an exact count is impossible. Sometimes fellow soldiers discovered their gender and they were immediately discharged. Many times, however, women fought entire battles with as much bravery and gusto as their male counterparts, never letting on that they were female.

》》》》》》》》》》》》》》》 ★ 《《《《《《《《《《《《《《《

children. Next in line and four years younger was her sister Emily Celestia. As the oldest, Rosetta had the most responsibility. She worked as a farmhand for her father, getting up early every morning and putting in long, hard hours doing chores. She also received some limited schooling, whereby she learned how to read and write, though she never did learn how to spell.

Rosetta grew strong mentally and physically, but she was dissatisfied with her life. Despite the fact that her father was also one of the constables in the nearby town of Afton, Rosetta's family was deeply in debt. Farms in the county were mostly dairy farms, but people grew corn, tobacco, and hops too—anything to try to make ends meet. However, no matter how hard Rosetta worked, the Wakeman family never seemed to have enough money.

With so many mouths to feed, 17-year-old Rosetta decided to get a job as a domestic servant. She was not on the job long before she realized she still would not earn enough money to help pull her family out of their financial difficulties. Money—or lack of it—was a constant problem and there was no end in sight.

This was not the life Rosetta wanted to lead. Surely there was something better for her in this world. One day she had an idea, and the more she thought about it, the more determined she became. She visited her favorite spotted calf one last time. She then put aside her dress and bonnet and put on a set of men's clothing. And she did one more thing: she took a pair of shears and lopped off her hair.

Rosetta traveled to nearby Binghamton, where she had no trouble getting a job. She earned $4 for two weeks' work, never letting on that her clear skin and beardless face were due to her gender more than her youth. For Rosetta's next job, she signed on as a boatman on the Chenango Canal, a section of water connecting the Susquehanna River in southern New York State to the Erie Canal up north. She would earn $20 for four trips.

Rosetta's very first trip on the canal changed the course of her life. In August 1862 she arrived in Canajoharie, a town of about 4,000 people. She met some soldiers there who urged her to enlist, thinking she was male. Joining up would offer unheard-of freedom and an unheard-of signing bonus: "I got when I enlisted 100 and 52$ in money." ($152—Rosetta's letters home were often riddled with mistakes in spelling, punctuation, and grammar.) Rosetta made a momentous decision. Claiming she was 21 years old, she agreed to serve in the Union army for three years. She knew she could do it. All she had to do was continue pretending she was a man.

On August 30 Rosetta joined the 153rd New York State Volunteers as Private Lyons Wakeman.

Mustered into service on October 17, 1862, Rosetta's regiment left the following day. Stationed in Alexandria, Virginia, for nine months, Rosetta's company set up camp across the river from Washington City. She looked around. Signs of the war were everywhere. Former churches, hotels, and even some private homes were now hospitals or government offices. Whole parks, once beautiful and well kept, now housed cattle or provided pens for pigs.

Sarah Rosetta Wakeman, a.k.a. Lyons Wakeman. *The Minerva Center, from An Uncommon Soldier*

Contrabands—formerly enslaved people—who sought refuge in the North helped to build entrenchments around the perimeter of the city.

Rosetta settled into her new life. Her company's orders were to bolster the defenses of the nation's capital. It was a prime target for the Confederate army, so there were heavy fortifications—tens of thousands of Union troops patrolled the region, residing in 118 forts and batteries. Expecting an attack at any time, Rosetta and her regiment spent many days and nights "awatching for the rebels." Rosetta boasted that she hoped they would come. "If they do, they will get lick." She practiced with her rifle and waited, though during her duty time, the Rebels never came.

Despite the hardships of war, Rosetta enjoyed her new life "first rate." She did well during the battle drills and was healthy and strong. With plenty of food—more than she ever counted on when back home—she felt like she was "getting fat as a hog." For the first time, Rosetta saw a chance to rise from the poverty of her childhood. She dreamed of her future. "If I ever own a farm It will be in Wisconsin. On the Prairie. I [am] enjoying my Self better this summer than I ever did before in this world."

Rosetta did not miss her impoverished life back home, but she did miss her family. She wrote frequent letters to them, proud that she could read and write well enough to do so. For the first time in her life, she had enough money and the means to earn more. She wanted more than anything to help her family get out of debt, and so she sent money home as often as she could. In her letters she wrote, "I believe that God will spare my life to come home once more. Then I will help you to pay you [your] debts. . . . When I get out of the service I will make money enough to pay all the debts that you owe." She promised her parents, "I will help you all I can as long as I live."

As uneventful as the guard duty in Alexandria could be, the rumble of cannons was never far off. Rosetta knew it was just a matter of time before the 153rd saw real action. Her company practiced over and over for the battlefield. Rosetta stood in the front rank while her comrades behind her loaded their guns and

RICH MAN'S WAR, POOR MAN'S BATTLE

When the Civil War began, nobody expected a long conflict. At first, men (and some women) on both sides volunteered to fight. In the North, President Abraham Lincoln initially called for 75,000 men to enlist for three months. But the war dragged on longer than anyone had anticipated, and each army needed many more soldiers. The South passed a law to draft men into service. A year later the North enacted a similar measure. Lincoln called for 300,000 men. If districts could not fill the quota, Congress would press men into service. However, in both the North and South, the draft laws had loopholes. For example, men could pay a fee (or provide a substitute) to exempt themselves from enlistment. The fee—$300 in the North (about $6,000 in today's dollars)—was beyond the ability of all but the rich to pay. Protests erupted in several cities. In New York City, mobs smashed and burned buildings, including a church, an orphanage, and the homes of several wealthy citizens. They also took their anger out on African Americans, who were not legally citizens and were therefore exempt from the draft. At the end of the city's four-day rampage, at least 105 people had been killed and many more were injured.

fired over her shoulder. She and the other soldiers worked hard. The officers in charge wanted to make sure that when they finally did go into battle, every man—and at least one woman—was ready.

That spring the 153rd expected to receive orders to move out. Rosetta was issued a better gun, an Enfield rifle, and three days' rations. However, the regiment did not leave right away as they had expected. When the orders finally came on July 20, 1863, Rosetta's company marched into Washington to provide security against any potential riots. There had been terrible violence in New York City and other places earlier that month. Protests had gotten out of hand when people demonstrated against conscription—forced enlistment—of men into the army. Officials feared that similar riots would spill over into Washington.

Despite the war, Washington remained a beautiful city. Rosetta's company moved into well-kept, two-story barracks near the Capitol Building that, though already in use by Congress, was still under construction. The rioting that accompanied the draft in other cities did not occur in Washington, even though every day more men were conscripted into the army. Here, the War Department drafted both African American and white men, but without the violence seen in other parts of the country. For Rosetta, the war was still some distance away, but not for long.

The war did seem far off—except when Rosetta was guarding Carroll Prison. The prison held enlisted Confederate soldiers as well as officers. There were also three female convicts, including two spies who had worked for the South. The third woman made the biggest impression on Rosetta. As soon as she could, Rosetta wrote another letter home: "One of them was a Major in the union army and she went into battle with her men. When the rebels bullets was acoming like a hail storm she rode her horse and gave orders to the men. Now She is in Prison for not doing accordingly to the regulation of war."

SLAVERY AND THE CIVIL WAR

By the 1800s many Americans questioned the practice of buying and selling human beings at the discretion of white slaveholders. These people, including President Abraham Lincoln, were called abolitionists. They wanted to abolish—get rid of—slavery. On April 6, 1859, Lincoln wrote in a letter, "He who would *be* no slave, must consent to *have* no slave."

There were many causes for the United States' Civil War, but the issue of slavery was one of the leading motives for the fight. During the war, African Americans served on both the Union and Confederate sides. However, in the Confederate army, black people were mostly cooks, stable hands, or other laborers. Historians agree that there may also have been a small number of black Confederate soldiers. On the other hand, about 10 percent of the soldiers in the Union army were black. Of the nearly 200,000 African American soldiers dressed in Union blue, up to half of them may have been formerly enslaved themselves.

When the war ended with victory by the North, it became officially illegal to "own" another person in the United States. The Thirteenth Amendment to the US Constitution states: "Neither slavery nor involuntary servitude, except as a punishment for crime whereof the party shall have been duly convicted, shall exist within the United States, or any place subject to their jurisdiction."

Rosetta worried about her own situation. She could not slip up even once. If any of the men she served with suspected she was a woman, Rosetta could be thrown into Carroll Prison too.

On February 18, 1864, the 153rd New York Volunteers were on the move. They marched to Alexandria to board the steam ship *Mississippi*. The nine days on the ship were a challenge for Rosetta. With little privacy, she had to be especially careful not to reveal her gender. It was a relief to finally land at Algiers in New Orleans, Louisiana. From there, Rosetta's company joined the Red River Campaign, a Union scheme to conquer the Confederate army in the region, as well as confiscate cotton from nearby plantations.

Over the next several days and weeks, Rosetta's regiment marched nearly 400 miles. They were deep into enemy territory now, and for the first time, her training was put to the test as skir-

mishes popped up along the way. Her company was directly involved in the Battle of Pleasant Hill, in which Rosetta fought bravely. In the end, though, it was not a Confederate bullet but disease that did her in. She was admitted to a field hospital on May 3, 1864, for acute diarrhea,

Sarah Rosetta Wakeman gravesite. *National Park Service*

a common complaint among soldiers of the time. When the condition did not get better, she traveled overland by wagon to a larger hospital in New Orleans. Rosetta entered Marine U.S.A. General Hospital on May 22. She died nearly a month later on June 19, 1864.

As far as the army knew, they were burying another male soldier when they dug Rosetta's gravesite in Chalmette National Cemetery near New Orleans. They marked the grave with a simple headstone: LYONS WAKEMAN, N.Y.

Rosetta's family did not forget her. They cherished her letters, keeping them safe for generations. When they finally shared this correspondence, the world was privileged to glimpse a brave, decent woman who defied convention to earn an honored place in history.

★ LEARN MORE ★

Courageous Women of the Civil War: Soldiers, Spies, Medics, and More by M. R. Cordell (Chicago: Chicago Review Press, 2016)
She Went to the Field: Women Soldiers of the Civil War by Bonnie Tsui (Guilford, CT: TwoDot, 2006)
An Uncommon Soldier: The Civil War Letters of Sarah Rosetta Wakeman, Alias Pvt. Lyons Wakeman, 153rd Regiment, New York State Volunteers, 1862–1864 by Sarah Rosetta Wakeman, edited by Lauren Cook Burgess (Pasadena, MD: Minerva Center, 1994)

Cathay Williams

Buffalo Woman

The morning was chilly, and it was a good thing too. Cathay could wear the baggy layers of men's clothing without suspicion.

Am I sure? She asked herself for the umpteenth time.

She was.

Cathay buttoned her man's jacket. She would leave her skirt and blouse behind. If things went as planned, she would not be needing them again for a very long time. Cathay stood up. Her height—five feet, nine inches—was a real advantage. She practiced walking once more, laying her feet down firmly and resisting the urge to sway her hips. The breeches she had borrowed from a friend felt strange but comfortable and oddly liberating too.

"Good morning," she tried saying aloud using a gruff voice.

She touched her newly shorn hair, peering into the looking glass. *It'll do*, she thought finally. Before she lost her nerve,

Cathay set out for Jefferson Barracks, the largest US military post west of the Mississippi.

The idea for enlisting—illegally—in the all-male army had come to her one night after an exhausting day of washing clothes and cooking. Now that the Civil War had ended, Cathay had a plan: she intended to become a soldier in the US Regular Army. And she knew she could do it too—at least the work part of it. Born into the grueling and demeaning life of a slave, Cathay was no stranger to hard work and difficult living conditions.

There were just two main challenges: Cathay was African American, and she was a woman. Still, once the idea had taken root, it would not let go. And she was lucky she lived close to Jefferson Barracks. For the first time in history, African American men could volunteer as professional soldiers of the US Regular Army. Maybe all those white veterans of the Civil War could go back to their homes and jobs, but for former slaves, there was no home to go back *to*. A job in the army offered protection, pay, and a chance for something better. It was an opportunity Cathay did not want to miss. She was not about to let the fact that she was a woman stop her.

She explained later, "I wanted to make my own living and not be dependent on relations or friends."

Cathay quickened her pace. On November 15, 1866, she walked with firm determination to the Jefferson Barracks recruitment office. She was strong and fit, and she would make a fine soldier. If only the army would give her that chance.

Cathay's experience in the Civil War bolstered her courage. After all, she had served in the Union army for nearly three and a half years, though not as a soldier. However, even as a washerwoman and cook, she had marched behind the troops and experienced the same poor living conditions. Sometimes she had a tent to sleep in, but often she had slept on the ground and out

《《《《《《《《《《《《《《《《《《《《《《《《《《《《《《《 ★ 》》》》》》》》》》》》》》》》》》》》》》》》》》》》》

A CALL TO MILITARY DUTY

Approximately 200,000 African American soldiers fought in the Civil War. When the war was over, there was still rampant discrimination against these brave soldiers, even in the highest ranks of government. However, after much argument, Congress agreed to create six all–African American units in the Regular Army. The country needed soldiers to serve on its western frontier. On July 28, 1866, President Andrew Johnson signed a landmark bill. For the first time in American history, African American units were formed into separate companies—two cavalry and four infantry.

Many men who'd been previously enslaved decided to enlist. The life of a soldier promised—but often did not deliver—shelter, regular meals, medical care, pay (a private was paid $13 a month), and honor, though racial prejudice frequently threatened the honor. The job included maintaining security for settlers in the West and assisting in westward expansion. These regiments were nicknamed Buffalo Soldiers, a respectful term given to them by Native Americans. Despite the reality of harsh living conditions, these soldiers served admirably. They had the lowest desertion rate of all the army's frontier units.

《《《《《《《《《《《《《《《《《《《《《《《《《《《《《《《 ★ 》》》》》》》》》》》》》》》》》》》》》》》》》》》》》

in the open. She had eaten the same bland hardtack and pork as the soldiers. Also, as a washerwoman she had been responsible for bringing along her equipment. There were two heavy wooden tubs, a scrub board and soap, and various other items. Whenever the camp moved, she had to find a wagon to carry her things—or haul them herself. Her life experiences, both while enslaved and while serving in the army, had made her independent, tough, and strong.

Now, Cathay paused outside the recruitment station, an unassuming stone building where she hoped to change her life. Then she stepped inside.

It was not hot inside, but Cathay began to sweat. However, she did not dare take off any of her layers of clothing. Instead, she strode over to the recruiter and told him that she wanted to join the infantry. She did not say so, but she did not know how to ride a horse, so the cavalry was out.

"Name?" the man's bored voice responded. He gave her a quick glance.

Cathay had already figured out the man's name she would use, a clever inversion of her own. "William," she replied, "William Cathay."

The officer wrote her name, not bothering to ask her to spell it. Cathay would not have been able to anyway—she had never had the opportunity to learn her letters.

"Age?" the man asked next.

"Twenty-two," Cathay gulped. She cleared her throat and answered the rest of the questions using a voice she hoped did not sound feminine. Major Henry Merriam signed the enlistment form. So far Cathay's plan had succeeded without a hitch.

"The surgeon will examine you now."

"Oh!" This time, Cathay let out a less-than-male-sounding squeak. Surely her secret would be revealed now. Would she be arrested for trying to enlist as a woman? What would her punishment be? With trembling knees, she stood waiting for the doctor, C. M. Powers, to discover her gender.

Cathay need not have worried. The doctor appeared even more bored than the major had been. He looked her up and

Cathay Williams, the only woman Buffalo Soldier in the US Army,
1866–1868. *The US Army website*

down and signed the form, declaring her "free from all bodily
defects and mental infirmary, which would, in any way, disqual-
ify him from performing the duties of a soldier."

"What's that?"

"Welcome to the United States Army, Private."

Cathay was now a member of the 38th United States Infantry, Company A, under Captain Charles Clarke.

Years later, Cathay shared her story with a newspaper reporter who, curious about a woman in the army, had asked to interview her. The reporter carefully recorded the details of Cathay's incredible life and, on January 2, 1876, published an article about her in the *St. Louis Daily Times*.

《《《《《《《《《《《《《《《《《《《《《《《《 ★ 》》》》》》》》》》》》》》》》》》》》》》》》

I DO SOLEMNLY SWEAR

By successfully enlisting on November 15, 1866, Cathay Williams became the first documented African American female to serve in the US Army. She, like the other recruits, was required to take an oath. The oath was written on her enlistment papers:

> *I, William Cathay, do solemnly swear, that I will bear true faith and allegiance to the United States of America, and that I will serve them honestly and faithfully against all their enemies or opposers whomsoever; and that I will observe and obey the orders of the President of the United States, and the orders of the officers appointed over me, according to the Rules and Articles of War.*

From 1866 to 1891, approximately 5,000 African American soldiers took this oath. They made up about 10 percent of the army's total strength.

《《《《《《《《《《《《《《《《《《《《《《《《 ★ 》》》》》》》》》》》》》》》》》》》》》》》》

Cathay had been born in September 1844 in a slave cabin near Independence in Jackson County, Missouri. Her father was a free man, but her mother was enslaved by a wealthy farmer named William Johnson. Her parents never married—it was illegal for them to do so.

During the Civil War, Union troops freed Cathay, though they promptly conscripted her to work as a washerwoman and cook.

Most incredibly, Cathay enlisted with the US Army in an infantry unit on the country's western frontier and served for two years before her gender was discovered.

Cathay remembered the spring of 1861 when Union soldiers swept into Cole County and through her hometown of Jefferson City, Missouri. One day she was enslaved and then suddenly the next day she was not. Until that day, she had worked her whole life from sunup to sundown with no choice but to do what she was told. She worked mostly as a servant in the plantation own-

er's house but may also have had to help in the fields when needed. She never expected to leave her current situation or gain the freedom to make her own life choices. That is, until the Civil War happened.

Cathay Williams.
Wikimedia Commons

〈〈〈〈〈〈〈〈〈〈〈〈〈〈〈〈〈〈〈〈〈〈〈〈〈〈〈〈 ★ 〉〉〉〉〉〉〉〉〉〉〉〉〉〉〉〉〉〉〉〉〉〉〉〉〉〉〉〉

THE EMANCIPATION PROCLAMATION

Effective January 1, 1863, President Abraham Lincoln signed into law a momentous proclamation. Up until that day, African American men, women, and children could legally be bought and sold as if they were no more than things rather than people. The Emancipation Proclamation, though limited in many ways and applicable to only certain parts of the country, made slavery a crime against the state. The proclamation stated, "And by virtue of the power, and for the purpose aforesaid, I do order and declare that all persons held as slaves within said designated States, and parts of States, are, and henceforward shall be free."

Though fought for a variety of complex reasons, the US Civil War divided the country on the issue of slavery. The Union North, also called the Federals, sought to abolish slavery. The South, the Confederates or "Rebels," wanted to maintain the legal right to use slave labor. In late spring of 1861, blue-clad Union soldiers under General Nathaniel Lyon marched into the Confederate Jackson City. They took the city without a fight as the governor, Claiborne Fox Jackson, and the rest of his government had already fled. The enslaved people there were declared free but promptly pressed into service for the Union army—often against their will.

〈〈〈〈〈〈〈〈〈〈〈〈〈〈〈〈〈〈〈〈〈〈〈〈〈〈〈〈 ★ 〉〉〉〉〉〉〉〉〉〉〉〉〉〉〉〉〉〉〉〉〉〉〉〉〉〉〉〉

Three months after the Union's takeover of Jackson City, the newly formed 8th Indiana Volunteer Infantry passed through, staying about a week. Cathay's life was forever changed. The army needed workers, and Cathay and other newly freed slaves soon found themselves drafted into service. She was assigned to be a cook and washerwoman, even though she had no experience cooking.

The regiment traveled extensively, seeking out Confederate forces. Cathay marched along with them. She was with the 8th Indiana during the Battle of Pea Ridge. She marched through Louisiana during the Red River Campaign and watched as Union soldiers burned enemy gunboats. At times conditions in the ranks were abysmal—food and supplies were frequently scarce, and disease picked off more of the troops than Confederate bullets.

Cathay was probably shocked when she received a new assignment. She was to cook and wash clothes for the officers of General Philip Sheridan's headquarters, the new commander of the division. One morning at dawn, she was right in the middle of things when Rebel troops launched a surprise attack.

On October 19, 1864, Cathay and Union soldiers were camped in the Shenandoah Valley. When the group was barely awake, the noise of battle erupted in the morning stillness. A panicked mass of Union soldiers retreated. With them, Cathay ran for her life. If she were caught, she would be sold to a wealthy landowner in the Deep South and forced to live as a slave once again. Fortunately for her, that never happened. General Sheridan was able to rally his soldiers and turn the near defeat into a resounding victory for the Union.

The Civil War ended in May 1865. The company Cathay was attached to was mustered out of service the following fall, on September 17, 1865. Cathay traveled to Missouri and settled near Jefferson Barracks. There her life took its most incredible twist yet, when she enlisted with the Buffalo Soldiers.

A man at the Jefferson Barracks handed Cathay a blue "Zouave" uniform and a Springfield rifle-musket. She changed into the clothing away from the rest of the men and then joined her new regiment. She felt the brass buttons on the dark blue jacket. They were stamped with the wings of an American eagle outstretched behind a shield. She wished she had a mirror, sure that she looked thoroughly impressive, but quickly shook her head. A man, she reasoned, would not show such vanity in front of others.

Cathay knew she had much to learn and that she would have to be very, very careful. *As long as nobody gives me away, I can keep this secret. I can be a soldier,* Cathay told herself. Two others knew her secret: a cousin and a "particular friend," both also members of the 38th. Cathay trusted that neither would give her away. Now she just needed to become an excellent soldier.

Company A consisted of 75 men (and one of them a woman!). Cathay was eager to get to work. However, soon after enlisting, she got sick. She had contracted smallpox and spent several months under medical care in St. Louis. Amazingly, her gender remained a secret during the hospitalization.

Once recovered from the smallpox, Cathay was ordered to Fort Riley, Kansas, where she reported for duty in April 1867. She then participated in a number of missions, marching hundreds of miles from one military outpost to another. When she arrived at Fort Cummings, New Mexico, the fort was the most desolate and dangerous Cathay had experienced yet. Danger here took many forms. The environment was harsh at this desert post. In addition, there was the constant threat of raids by the Apache people, who had been driven from their lands. Perhaps worst, though, was the unexpected racism. The white officers at Fort Cummings often treated Cathay's unit harshly and unfairly.

To top it off, conditions here were poor at best. There was a lack of quality food, adequate clothing, or even clean shelter.

These factors may have contributed to further health problems for Cathay. She was in and out of the infirmary, though miraculously she was still able to conceal the fact that she was a woman. Cathay endured a number of ailments including scabies, rheumatism, and neuralgia (a condition causing intense pain due to nerve damage). Finally, after a grim and nearly thankless service, Cathay decided to terminate her army career. She allowed the doctor to discover she was a woman.

Cathay's discharge papers were dated October 14, 1868. Her commander wrote, "He is unable to do military duty. . . . This condition dates prior to enlistment."

When the men in her unit found out Cathay was a woman, some of them treated her "real bad." But Cathay was a survivor. She knew how to take care of herself, and so it was with dignity and resolve that she left the army to get on with her life.

Cathay spent the rest of her years in the American frontier, though she moved several times before she finally settled down in Trinidad, Colorado. Conditions for an independent African American woman were better in the West than in other parts of the country. There was a large community of people who had been enslaved, as well as a mixture of other races. Cathay used her skills as a cook and laundress to eventually earn enough money to purchase her own wagon and team of horses. With this success, she married—briefly and disastrously. Her husband "was of no account," and she had him arrested for stealing nearly everything of value she owned. She did not remarry but lived out her days determined and independent.

It was only when Cathay was plagued by health issues again—this time it was diabetes, and her toes had to be amputated—that she sought help from the government. Now an invalid, she applied for a pension. Others, even women, had been granted military pensions for their military service. The army denied Cathay twice.

Historians are unsure when exactly Cathay died or where she was buried. Over a century after she passed away, destitute and forgotten, Cathay's great service to this country was finally recognized and honored. Today, her story is a cherished piece of US history. In 2016 a bronze statue to honor Cathay was erected in Leavenworth, Kansas. If she were alive today, she would no doubt be proud of her legacy that helped elevate the status of women in the military.

★ LEARN MORE ★

Buffalo Soldiers Research Museum, www.buffalosoldiersre scarchmuseum.org/default.htm

Cathy Williams: From Slave to Female Buffalo Soldier by Phillip Thomas Tucker (Mechanicsburg, PA: Stackpole Books, 2002)

PART II

The World at War

World War I and World War II

★ ★ ★ ★ ★

RESOURCEFUL, VERSATILE, AND SPEEDY RECRUITS SENT ACROSS WATER TO WORK UNDER HAZARDOUS CONDITIONS read the Washington, DC, *Evening Star* newspaper headline on May 19, 1918. The recruits were female telephone operators, nicknamed "Hello Girls" because their job was to manually connect calls using a switchboard. This cutting-edge technology during World War I gave army commanders the ability to communicate quickly with troops and was critical to their success in battle.

Seven months earlier, on October 8, 1917, General "Black Jack" Pershing sent an urgent cable. The American Expeditionary Force (AEF) in France desperately needed 100 female bilingual telephone operators, he wrote. The women, he explained, would be working at switchboards throughout the country, some perilously close to enemy lines. The AEF had already tried using male service members and even French women, but these workers did not have the necessary skills. Back in the United States, thousands of women responded to advertisements in newspapers around the country, but only a select few who were fluent in both French and English qualified. These women wore dark blue army uniforms—which they were required to purchase themselves at significant cost—and sailed across the Atlantic. Several were stationed directly behind the trenches where Allies fought against enemy forces. "Number, please," they repeated hundreds of times each day as they connected calls that relayed sensitive and often classified information.

As important as the Hello Girls' work had been to the success of World War I, when they were no longer needed overseas and these women returned home, the army did not recognize them as service members. They were retroactively labeled "civilian contractors." It was not until decades later that they were given army status and official recognition. Still, the part these and other women played during this period in history helped pave the way for the advancement of the women who followed.

American telephone girls on arrival in France, 1918. *US Army Women's Museum, Fort Lee, Virginia*

Like a ripple in a pond, the idea for a permanent Women's Army Corps started with little momentum, despite women's vital contributions to conflict after conflict. While Congress had established the Army Nurse Corps in 1901, it was not until World War II that the army launched an official all-female, non-medical force.

World War II was looming in 1940. The United States was not officially in the war until after the Japanese bombing of Pearl Harbor on December 7, 1941, but Americans could see that direct engagement was just a matter of time. After the Pearl Harbor attack, the whisper of war became a battle cry, and along with it came a call for women to "Free a Man to Fight." President Franklin Roosevelt signed Public Law 554 on May 15, 1942, establishing the Women's Army Auxiliary Corps (WAAC) with the idea that women would take over noncombatant support jobs from men. The new law stated, "I do hereby establish a Women's Army Auxiliary Corps for non-combatant service with the Army of the United States for the purpose of further making available to the national defense the knowledge, skill, and special training of the women of this Nation." (A year later, the army dropped the "auxiliary" status and founded the Women's Army Corps—WAC.) Now the WAAC just needed a director to head this newly formed army branch.

Oveta Culp Hobby was a woman renowned for her energy and good ideas. She would be perfect for the job. The only problem was that she had politely declined. She had young children and a job, she explained, and felt needed at home. Before the WAAC became official, Oveta received a phone call one Sunday evening. It was General Alexander Surles, director of the bureau of public relations in the War Department. He asked her to help set up a women's interest section in the War Department. The first time he had asked had been the week before. After the

Oveta Culp Hobby at her swearing-in ceremony. *US Army Women's Museum, Fort Lee, Virginia*

phone call, Oveta talked with her husband—and dialed the general back. Duty called, and Oveta agreed to take the job on a temporary basis.

The next step was the WAAC. This time, the army's chief of staff, General George Marshall, recommended just one person to become its first director: Oveta Hobby. Since there was no female equivalent of an army uniform yet, Oveta wore her own fancy hat and white gloves to her swearing-in ceremony on May 15, 1942.

The WAAC—and later WAC—was more than a good idea. It was the beginning of a revolution and proved critical to winning the war. Over 150,000 women served in the WAC during World War II, including 6,000 officers. Despite its success, the acceptance of women into the army was not always an easy transition. Women had to fight against discrimination and the doubts of many of their male counterparts. Charity Adams, the first African American woman commissioned as an officer, had to fight racial discrimination as well. Yet Charity proved her worth throughout her tenure in the army. She commanded the 6888th Central Postal Directory Battalion in both England and France during World War II. Indeed, women all over the United States answered the call for military service. When Japanese fighters bombed her beloved Oʻahu in Hawaiʻi, Margaret KC Yang was among the first of the island's women to enlist.

The plan for women to serve in the army was in motion. Numbers swelled—as did increasingly challenging duties. Yet, with the end of World War II, the WAC was set to expire on June 30, 1948. To ensure that females could continue serving in the army, Congress passed the Women's Armed Service Integration Act in 1948. This gave women permanent military status and continued entitlement to veterans' benefits. In the decades that followed, the assimilation of women into previously all-male military roles accelerated. Over and over, women excelled at positions of tremendous responsibility in conflicts all over the world.

Grace Banker

Number, Please

On December 9, 1917, Grace Banker wrote a letter to the Signal Corps, the branch of the United States Army responsible for communications. "Dear Sir," she began. "In the New York Globe of December the fifth a notice appeared regarding the need of recruits for telephone service in France." Very much interested in the job, Grace explained that she could speak both English and French and that she was thoroughly trained in "telephony." When she did not hear back, Grace wrote a second letter. This time Grace received a response. Yes, the Signal Corps wanted her to work as a telephone operator for the army. And yes, she would be working close to the fighting lines in France.

March 6, 1918, was a gray day with a drizzling rain that cast a dismal blanket over the converted troopship. Twenty-five-year-old Grace was aboard the *Celtic*. There were 32 other women on the camouflaged ship ranging in age from 19 to 35. As chief operator, Grace was in charge of all of them.

Grace Banker, World War I. *US Army Women's Museum, Fort Lee, Virginia*

Now, Grace pressed her face to a porthole and watched as the Statue of Liberty faded from sight. She would have preferred to be on deck, but no one was allowed outside until they were far out to sea. Grace had no idea if they would sail straight to France or stop in England first. All she knew was that they were sailing in a convoy of several ships—it was safer that way. There were other precautions too. There were no flashlights allowed, no portholes open at night, and no music once the sun went down. The sound, the captain explained, might alert an unseen enemy ship. One more thing: there were lifeboat drills every morning at 10:30.

On March 16 the ship was off the coast of England, but it became stuck on a sandbar. Suddenly, security tightened even more. "We are well in to the danger zone now," Grace wrote in her diary. The likelihood of attack by a German U-boat (*Unterseeboot*—a submarine) was high. And if they *were* torpedoed, the chances for living through the experience were slim. After all, only a quarter of the passengers had survived when a U-boat had attacked the RMS *Lusitania*.

On that clear, moonlit night, Grace felt like a sitting duck.

For three nights Grace and the other passengers slept in their clothes. An escort of torpedo boats and destroyers gathered around them. "They look like a lot of skating bugs shooting hither and thither, now slipping under our bow, now suddenly popping up beside us and going through all sorts of weird maneuvers," she wrote. She hoped they would land soon—and that an enemy ship didn't sink them first.

Grace Banker grew up in New Jersey. She graduated from Barnard College in 1915 with a double major in history and French. From there, she took a job with American Telephone and Telegraph Company (AT&T) in New York City. She worked her way up to the Instructor Department of the company. Then one day she was reading the Sunday edition of the *New York Globe* when she came across an ad for recruits to operate switchboards in Europe. Grace wrote a letter to the War Department. At first her letter went unanswered. That did not stop Grace. She wrote a second letter and finally received an application. Yes, she had

GETTING THE MESSAGE THROUGH

The Signal Corps is the branch of the army responsible for communication. It was founded in 1860 when army doctor Albert J. Myer had a great idea for communicating over long distances. He invented a system of flag signals by daylight, and torch or lantern signals at night. Before this, couriers were the only way to relay messages. During World War I, men, homing pigeons, and even dogs carried sensitive messages from one location to another. (The dogs weren't always effective because nobody wanted to send them into danger.) The army also used radios, but these were bulky and could only transmit using Morse code—a series of long and short clicks representing each letter of the alphabet. Plus, enemies could often intercept the radio messages. Commanders needed a secure and effective means of communicating with their soldiers. The telephone was the answer. But there was a problem. There were few people in France who could efficiently work the complicated, high-paced switchboards.

experience with "telephony," she wrote on the form. Yes, she spoke French.

The army wrote her back. Grace was assigned an interview—and she was evaluated by the Intelligence Section. Those "Hello Girls" (telephone operators) chosen would be stationed in France, some directly behind enemy lines. They would be responsible for transmitting many classified messages over telephone wires. The army needed to determine Grace's loyalty and ability to work under pressure. Satisfied on both accounts, they offered Grace the job and she accepted. She would support the efforts of the American Expeditionary Forces (AEF) under General John Pershing, and her job was to be chief operator. Her salary was $125 per month.

When this first unit of telephone operators landed in England, Grace was wearing the navy blue uniform and cap she had been required to purchase herself. All the operators' uniforms included a white armband with insignia showing a blue outline of a telephone mouthpiece. Grace, as chief operator, had the same emblem, but with a wreath around it and blue lightning flashes coming from the telephone receiver. The gravity of her position weighed heavily on her. She was responsible for the conduct of every woman in her charge. She also knew that this work was critical—the ability to communicate effectively could change the course of the war.

In Liverpool, England, evidence of the war was everywhere. Most notable was the lack of able-bodied men. All over, women had taken over their jobs. There were other clues too. At the British Canteen Service, Grace was at first grateful to receive a steaming cup of coffee. But what a disappointment it turned out to be! It was a substitute—roasted barley, not coffee, and with saccharine instead of sugar. Grace tossed it out. She bustled with the others to the Liverpool train station, noting that even the railway yards were full of female workers.

Later Grace bought "chocolate" from a boy who had set up shop on the platform at one of the train stations they passed through. The brown squares certainly looked like chocolate, but they were bitter and not at all tasty. Grace saved hers for a souvenir. She did drink a cup of the sham coffee, though. *At least it was something hot*, she told herself. It took her longer to get used to the bread, impossible to bite into because it was so hard. She chipped off small pieces with a knife.

Grace and the others did not stay long in England. Soon they crowded aboard a Channel packet (a steamship designed to transport mail) called the *Normania*. Along with French civilians and soldiers from a variety of countries, Grace huddled around a smokestack to keep warm. They were sailing from Portsmouth to Le Havre, France, through waters crawling with German U-boats. Instead of a run-in with a submarine, however, a French destroyer nearly rammed them, unable to clearly identify them in the dark and fog.

Luckily, they landed safely and bustled aboard a train. En route to Paris, Grace opened her army rations: one can each of beans, tomatoes, and cheese—all cold—along with hardtack (a type of hard, dry biscuit) in a paper box. Since there were no eating utensils, she used the paper box to form a makeshift spoon. She ate everything except the tomatoes.

In Paris the operators split into three groups. Grace's unit left for Chaumont sur Haute Marne, a military barracks near the front lines of the war that was the headquarters of commander General Pershing. Grace got to work.

"When a line signal is received, plug into the answering jack with a back cord and say, 'Number Please?'"

"Where directories have been furnished, if the call is by name, say, 'What is the number please?'"

The military phone regulations that Grace had memorized were fresh in her mind. While in training in the United States, she had been confident that she could keep everything straight, even when the switchboard got busy. But now the rules and regulations buzzed around her like artillery on the front lines. "Conversation on long distance calls over A.E.F. lines are limited to six minutes," she recited. But then she added, "excepting between the hours of 12:00 noon and 2:00 PM and 7:00 PM and 9:00 AM." Of course, this rule was different when the calls were over French lines. The hours were the same, but the maximum time allowed was 15 minutes. And that was subject to change. Or another: "If no answer is received after the first ring, continue to ring about every 10 seconds for a period of 90 seconds."

It was a lot to keep track of.

Nevertheless, Grace was satisfied with her work, though the days were long and tiring. Calls flew in, many critical to the survival of the men fighting from trenches a few short miles away. Grace loved it when she spoke with an incredulous male voice on the other end of the lines. "Are you American Girls? Gee but it's good to hear your voice." One man exclaimed, "When you said 'Number please,' I couldn't answer, there was a lump in my throat."

The telephone office was a two-mile trek from where the telephone girls were staying in beautiful Chaumont with its

Long-distance toll office near La Belle Epine, outside of Paris. *US Army Women's Museum, Fort Lee, Virginia*

《《《《《《《《《《《《《《《《《《《《《《《《《《《《《《《 ★ 》》》》》》》》》》》》》》》》》》》》》》》》》》》》》》》

CIRCUITS OF VICTORY

Author Abraham L. Lavine called the telephones of World War I "Circuits of Victory." When Alexander Graham Bell took out a patent for his telephone invention in 1876, no one could predict what a crucial role the telephone would play. During the Great War—1914 to 1918—linemen placed lightweight telephone wire across hundreds of miles throughout Europe. These first systems required an operator to connect calls. While the caller simply had to lift the receiver from a candlestick-shaped instrument, the operator's job was more complicated. She had to first plug in the jack associated with the call and then determine how to connect it. If the call was within the immediate network, the operator plugged the other end of the cord to the corresponding jack. She also had to remember to trip a switch so that the ringer would sound on the other end. Beyond the network, she had to call a long-distance operator who either connected the call herself or relayed the call to another operator even farther away. Depending on the distance, this series of transactions could take a long time. During World War I, operators placed thousands of top-secret calls. Since operators could listen in to any call, they had to be 100 percent loyal—and no gossiping allowed.

《《《《《《《《《《《《《《《《《《《《《《《《《《《《《《《 ★ 》》》》》》》》》》》》》》》》》》》》》》》》》》》》》》》

green meadows and first violets of the season. The commander in chief, General Pershing, was temporarily residing in an impressive nearby chateau. Despite the beauty, Grace could not forget there was a war going on. She wrote in her diary, "We are told to keep our mouths shut, ask no questions, and never

discuss anything." Officers and enlisted men crowded Chaumont's crooked streets. Ambulance after ambulance rushed the
wounded to the nearby hospital.

Midmorning on August 25, 1918, Grace was directed to go
home and pack. She received new orders in the car that came to
pick her up. Grace and four other operators were to report to the
telephone office in Ligny-en-Barrois, a town close to the fighting
front. They arrived that evening.

"All night long the streets of Ligny gave back the sound of
marching feet and the camions [military trucks] and artillery
added their rumble." Here, Grace's room was over an old barn
stacked with herbs, tables, and clocks. Her room held a surpris-
ingly ornate canopied bed. Portraits of its previous occupants
and a cross of dried flowers hung on the wall.

The telephone office, banked with sandbags, was in a house
in the center of town. Inside were three switchboards and no
other furniture. Grace used a packing box for a chair and desk.
Security here was tight. Instead of using actual names, callers
substituted code words such as *waterfall* for Ligny or *Nemo* for
the 4th Corps. The code words changed constantly too. More
than ever, Grace felt the urgency and importance of her work.
If commanders could communicate with soldiers on the front
lines, lives could be saved.

Grace could sense that something big was about to happen.

The Battle of Saint-Mihiel took place from September 12 to
15. During the drive and in the days leading up to it, the operators worked day and night. On September 10, one of the officers
escorted Grace home at 11:30 at night. Bleary-eyed, she was back
at the office at 3:00 AM. The first wave of Allied soldiers was set to
attack an hour later. Grace connected calls nonstop. For two days
she functioned on two hours of sleep, but hardly noticed. When
her eye got infected, she barely paused to have it lanced.

All the work paid off. By the end of the offensive, Grace could tell that things had gone well. All at once, the voices over the lines were no longer strained and nervous. More and more captured soldiers streamed into the town's barbed wire enclosure, a holding camp for the prisoners of war. However, the respite was brief. Soon, Grace received orders to head to the next battlefront. This time she and the others followed the First Army to Souilly.

The operators' living quarters in Souilly were "flimsy wood affairs set down in the fields on the edge of the village." Their building, Barracks Number Eight, was primitive and cold. Oiled paper rather than glass covered the windows—and these pushed out like windows in a chicken coop. At night Grace helped cover them with a black cloth to prevent any light from seeping out and identifying their location to enemy aircraft. Beds, too, were primitive. The army cots were topped with straw mattresses and so narrow that she had to be careful when she turned over in her sleep. Grace hung her helmet and gas mask on the wall and settled in.

One day Grace was outside the barracks when an enemy airplane flew overhead. It reminded her of a harmless little dragonfly, and she paused to stare at it. Then, as an antiaircraft gun shot at it, puffs of smoke like cotton clouded the clear sky. Too late, Grace realized that the fired shrapnel would soon come down. She started for cover as the metal fragments rained around her, one piece landing directly next to her. She had not thought to wear her helmet.

The fighting here was close. Grace could hear the constant thud of bombs and guns. Flashes lit up the sky as the barracks shook from the impact of artillery a few miles away. The line of prisoners coming into camp was a slow but steady current, with many of them barely older than children. Grace mused in

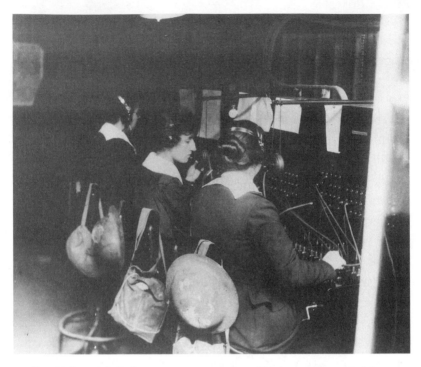

Hello Girls with helmets, France, 1918. *US Army Women's Museum, Fort Lee, Virginia*

her diary, "They tramp past our open door and gaze curiously at us. Suppose they wonder what we are doing here. We stare back at them just as curiously. That old bespectacled bean pole, I am sure has been a student of chemistry in a Bosche [slang for "German"] university, and that one a fisherman from the coast. 'Bah, they are all Bosches. And too well treated.'"

Despite the number of prisoners, resistance was still fierce. Grace thought of her only brother, Gene, whom she had not heard from for too long. Where was he? Was he OK? It seemed like the war would never end.

"Would you like to see the hospital or will it make you sick?" one of the officers asked Grace one day.

Inside the hospital the wounded waited their turn for help—
including several Germans. Grace did not expect to see such
horror, but the officer took her everywhere. In one of the operating rooms, a doctor's hand was buried in a man's chest as he
probed for a piece of artillery shell. *War is hell,* Grace told herself. *War is hell.* She refused the car ride back to the barracks. She
needed to walk. She needed to forget the things she had seen.

Workdays continued, long and frantic. Writing in her diary
provided Grace with an outlet.

Friday.

Saturday.

Raining as usual.

The sun has forgotten France.

When I get home I am going to sleep for a week without stopping,
Grace told herself.

Once Grace's feet froze when a leak in the roof dripped onto
her bed. She had been too exhausted to notice the wet blankets,
and so for two days she ignored the cold. By the third morning,
the problem was severe. Her feet swelled so badly that she could
not wear shoes for days. But she did not complain. She knew
she was far better off than the boys in the trenches. She worried
more about her brother and mailed off cigarettes to him, not
sure if they would ever reach him.

The fighting went on and on. As soldier after soldier trooped
through on their way to the front battle lines, Grace and the
others tried to boost their morale whenever they could take a
short break. "Hello boys! Three cheers! Yanks!" they yelled to
the men as they marched past.

New orders came in November. Grace was to move forward
again, this time to the next headquarters at Dun-sur-Meuse.

It did not happen. Instead, three days later, rumors flew
around the office that Germany was about to sign an armistice,

an agreement to end the war. Suddenly, on November 11, 1918, the 11th day of the 11th month, the war was over. Incredible! Grace could hardly believe it. After hearing the news, everyone was wild with excitement. A French sergeant from the office next door exclaimed in less than perfect English, "I could jump up and down and hit the ceiling." Grace knew exactly how he felt.

Overall, Grace spent 20 months serving in the US Army. In May 1919 she was awarded the Distinguished Service Medal for her efforts in leading the telephone operators. It was no doubt that their untiring aid had helped the Allies win the war.

In September 1919 Grace sailed for home. Once back in the States, she reunited with her family. Her brother, Gene, thank

Chief Operator Grace Banker (second row, far left) was awarded the Distinguished Service Medal at American Forces Headquarters, Coblenz, Germany, June 1919. *National Archives*

goodness, had also survived the war. Grace hung up her uniform and got on with her life, eventually getting married and having four children. Though she never forgot her experience in the war, there was one thing that rankled her: the army seemed to forget *her*. Once stateside, the War Department refused to acknowledge the Hello Girls as part of the armed forces. Downgraded to civilian volunteers, this position was not rectified until decades later. When Congress finally granted the Hello Girls military status in 1977, Grace never knew it. She had died on September 17, 1960, at the age of 67.

★ LEARN MORE ★

Circuits of Victory by A. Lincoln Lavine (Garden City, NY: Doubleday, Page, 1921)

The Hello Girls: America's First Women Soldiers by Elizabeth Cobbs (Cambridge, MA: Harvard University Press, 2017)

Oveta Culp Hobby

The Little Colonel

Oveta Culp Hobby—*Colonel* Oveta Culp Hobby—stood at the lectern and looked out over the audience. Sitting under the trees were 436 newly commissioned third officers. Though all were wearing the uniform of the Women's Army Auxiliary Corps (WAAC), the women were missing one thing. The insignia of the WAACs, featuring the goddess Pallas Athene, had been ordered, but delivery was late. No matter. Despite the missing insignia, it was a perfect day for graduation, sunny with a slight breeze. Yes, it was an incredible, historic day. How much had been accomplished since that rainy May 16, 1942, when Oveta had been sworn in to office. How hard she and everyone had worked to create a viable force of women who would directly aid in the efforts of the war.

Oveta, at five feet, four inches tall, had been dubbed by some the "Little Colonel," but today she had never felt taller—or more proud of the uniform she was wearing. It used to be that she did not give a hang about clothes (at least according to her father), but that had changed. Now she stood quietly in her neatly pressed olive-drab jacket and skirt, her "Hobby" hat firm on her head with her hair tucked crisply underneath. Today Oveta was addressing the very first officers in the WAAC!

"Your graduation today, in a real sense, is a commencement of service. From here on your way must be the long, hard road to Victory. No one can forecast what this war will bring. I can give you no promise as to what lies ahead of you. I *can* assure you that you will be serving the purpose you had in mind when you volunteered as Officer Candidates in the WAAC."

Not everyone had welcomed this day, and not all could be counted on to smooth the way for the future of the WAAC. Ever since Congresswoman Edith Nourse Rogers—here for today's ceremony—had introduced the bill to the US Congress, there had been pockets of fierce resistance to the idea of women serving in the army. Some said the women were "embarrassing the War Department." Others made jokes, calling the women "Wackies" or the "Petticoat Army." One reporter declared the WAAC a "serious menace to the home and foundation of a true Christian and democratic country." Ever since she had taken this job, Oveta was especially careful about what she said or did. She knew this experiment would determine the future of women in the army for years to come.

Oveta stepped from the lectern. She felt a flush of gratitude for General George C. Marshall, Chief of Staff of the Army, a man who *was* a supporter of women in the army. She smiled, thinking of his note to her. He had written about the confidence he felt for the future of the WAAC and remarked, "This is only the beginning of a magnificent war service by the women of America."

Oveta felt that way too. She just needed to make sure everything *worked*.

(Left to right) Major General Ulio, Hobby, and Colonel Donald Faith
review the first graduating class, 1942. *US Army Women's Museum,
Fort Lee, Virginia*

Oveta was born on January 19, 1905, in Killeen, Texas, a
town of a few hundred people in the middle of the state. She
came from a prosperous family, the second daughter of seven
children and one of two families in the area that owned an auto-
mobile. Oveta was heavily influenced by her parents. Her father
was a lawyer, a twice-elected official to the Texas House of Representatives, and an ordained Baptist preacher. Oveta's mother,
Emma, was also politically minded. Once she instructed young
Oveta and her sister to can peaches while she went out cam-
paigning for the man running for governor, Oveta's future husband, William Hobby. William had helped get women the right
to vote in Texas, and Emma was out to make sure women were
taking advantage of the opportunity.

《《《《《《《《《《《《《《《《《《《《《《《《《《《《《《《《 ★ 》》》》》》》》》》》》》》》》》》》》》》》》》》》》》》》》

WAAC BEGINNINGS

Canada, Britain, and the Soviet Union had already incor-
porated women into their war efforts by the time World War
II began. Besides the Nurse Corps, the US Army, Navy, and
Marines had hired only a few hundred women during World
War I and had no provisions (future plans) for wide-scale
use of women in the military.

The War Department dragged its feet about this issue
until 1941, when three people in particular helped to push
forward the idea of a Women's Army Auxiliary Corps: First
Lady Eleanor Roosevelt; the army chief of staff, George C.
Marshall; and Congresswoman Edith Nourse Rogers. On
May 28, 1941, Congresswoman Rogers introduced a bill
to the House of Representatives. She wanted women to
serve in the army and to receive the same benefits as men.
She had to compromise. The WAAC would serve *with* the
army, but it would not be a
part of the army. While Congress debated the bill for
nearly a year, General Marshall directed a pre-planning
committee to work out some
of the details for a corps of
women volunteers.

**First Lady Eleanor Roosevelt
(left) and Oveta Culp Hobby,
Fort Des Moines, 1944.** *Anna
Lawrence Scarry Collection, Wom-
en's Memorial Foundation Collection*

《《《《《《《《《《《《《《《《《《《《《《《《《《《《《《《《 ★ 》》》》》》》》》》》》》》》》》》》》》》》》》》》》》

To those who knew Oveta, there was no doubt that she was tenacious and driven. In sixth grade, there was a spelling contest at school. The prize for the year-long contest was a brand-new Bible. Young Oveta assured her teacher from the beginning, "You might as well put my name on that Bible right now." At the end of the year Oveta, as she had predicted, earned the prize.

Oveta excelled in many areas. For one, she was a gifted speaker, despite stammering as a child. She practiced her public speaking in a friend's backyard, preaching her own sermons to a group of neighborhood children. She continued to hone this skill, taking elocution lessons in high school and participating in debates and dramatics. She once recited a poem called "Alaska, the Brave Cowgirl" and was offered a position with a group of traveling performers. Oveta was disappointed—her parents wouldn't hear of letting her go.

WOMEN'S INTEREST SECTION

In October 1940 the War Department began drafting men ages 21 to 35 into the US Army. By June 1941, with the country inching closer to war, mothers, sisters, wives, and sweethearts flooded the War Department with thousands of letters every day. They wanted to know what they could do to support the war effort. They wanted information about their men. General Alexander Day Surles was the director of public affairs for the army. He realized that the War Department needed a way to appropriately handle these inquiries. He asked Oveta Culp Hobby to lead a Women's Interest Section. This organization set the stage for the formation of the WAAC soon to follow.

Not to be deterred, Oveta organized her own theater group. She and her friends called themselves the Jolly Entertainers and gave performances for charity.

Oveta's family and friends called her brilliant. At the age of 10, she read her father's copy of the Congressional Record. By the time she was 13, she had read the entire Bible three times. Despite Oveta's intelligence—or maybe because school did not offer her enough of a challenge—she did not graduate from high school. And, though she attended some classes at Mary Hardin-Baylor College and the University of Texas law school, she did not earn a degree from either. She certainly never had any intention of joining the army—not that she could have if she wanted to. Women were not allowed to be soldiers until Oveta helped to make that happen 15 years later. As she grew up, Oveta had no idea that everything she did was preparing her to be one of the most influential women of her generation.

Oveta worked in politics and in the newspaper business. Six days before her 21st birthday she took a position as a parliamentarian of the Texas House of Representatives, the first woman ever to do so. Her job was to ensure that proper rules and procedures were followed during each session of parliament. She also campaigned for a seat in the Texas legislature. (She lost, but it was close.) She married William Hobby, then a newspaper editor and president of the *Houston Post-Dispatch*, and later had two children, both delivered by Caesarian section on January 19, her own birthday. While working at the newspaper and on various committees and boards, she wrote a book entitled *Mr. Chairman* about parliamentary law. It seemed there was nothing Oveta Culp Hobby could not do.

One Sunday during dinner, the phone rang at the home of Oveta and William Hobby. Oveta excused herself to answer it. She came back to the table a few minutes later and told her husband that the caller was General Alexander Day Surles. She explained that he wanted her to go to Washington to lead a women's interest section for the army. She told him again that she couldn't possibly. After all, she reasoned, she had a family and a newspaper business to take care of.

Again? The general had *already* asked her once? William asked his wife to reconsider. With a war going on, everyone had a duty to serve. Oveta called General Surles back. She offered her services for four months.

Oveta resigned from the army four *years* later.

On May 16, 1942, Oveta chose her outfit with care. It would have been better if her army uniform was ready, but that would take another month. So, she chose a collared dress, white gloves, and a particularly nice wide-brimmed hat. As she stood with her right hand raised, Major General Myron C. Cramer swore her in as director of the Women's Army Auxiliary Corps. The WAAC was real! Oveta could hardly believe it.

As soon as the ceremony was over, Oveta hit the ground running. She had already traveled to Canada and England to learn how those countries had organized their own women's corps. In the States, she had been involved in the WAAC pre-planning committee, anticipating that the law for a women's army corps would pass soon. Now she made a mental list of the things she needed to do immediately:

- ▶ Oversee recruitment efforts, ensuring that the 25,000 slots were filled (this was later changed to 150,000 slots).

- ▶ Prepare a location for the women to train, and make sure that all equipment, including uniforms, was delivered on time.

❱❱ Help select the candidates for the first class of WAAC officers.

At first, Oveta received requests from prominent citizens who felt they should be given direct appointments as officers. "No," she repeated again and again. All WAAC officers would need to *earn* that position, having met all requirements at the officer training school. Oveta shocked those around her by announcing that she, too, would attend the training school. General Marshall firmly nixed her plan. That was not army protocol, he explained.

But who *would* be chosen for this first class? One newspaper reported, "Women will be selected with extreme care, for their experience, special abilities, and moral character."

Recruitment offices opened for WAACs on May 27, 1942. All over the country, thousands of women applied, and the recruiting offices desperately called for more application forms. Nearly 140,000 forms were given to prospective WAACs. The first day alone, 13,208 women filled out the forms. *How on earth will we choose only 440 women?* Oveta thought. Who they chose was critically important. These women would make—or break—the future of the WAAC.

When her uniform finally arrived in June, Oveta set aside her personal wardrobe. In uniform, she reported to General Marshall, who promptly directed her to wear a set of colonel's eagles on her shoulder, though her official promotion came later. Her colleagues were not surprised. As *Time* magazine stated, "Even if Oveta Culp Hobby had started as a Private, she would have become the Colonel anyhow."

Oveta wore the uniform constantly as she traveled all over the country to speak to various groups about the WAAC. Because she had only one uniform, she brought along an electric

〈〈〈〈〈〈〈〈〈〈〈〈〈〈〈〈〈〈〈〈〈〈〈〈〈〈〈〈〈〈〈 ★ 〉〉〉〉〉〉〉〉〉〉〉〉〉〉〉〉〉〉〉〉〉〉〉〉〉〉〉〉〉〉〉

LEADING LADIES, BUT NO PRIMA DONNAS

"Enrollment in the Corps is voluntary and open to all women, regardless of race, creed, or color, married or single, citizens of the United States by birth or naturalization."

When Oveta spoke to a sorority at Howard University on July 6, 1942, she explained how 440 officer candidates, including 40 African American women, had been chosen from the more than 30,000 "blanks" (application forms) turned in. For this first class of officers, women were required to have at least a high school education or equivalent, and most were between the ages of 21 and 45. They had passed a physical exam and had scored well on a mental alertness exam, a test similar to the one given to male recruits. Despite a rigorous interview, there were still 4,000 potential candidates.

"Director's Representatives," 19 women (including Mary McLeod Bethune advocating for the African American women to be chosen) and a team of psychiatrists worked hard to whittle down the list. On Saturday, June 27, Oveta and her team pored over every application. Finally, on the evening of June 30, Oveta declared the list complete. Now there was less than a month to prepare for the WAAC candidates to arrive at Fort Des Moines, Iowa.

〈〈〈〈〈〈〈〈〈〈〈〈〈〈〈〈〈〈〈〈〈〈〈〈〈〈〈〈〈〈〈 ★ 〉〉〉〉〉〉〉〉〉〉〉〉〉〉〉〉〉〉〉〉〉〉〉〉〉〉〉〉〉〉〉

fan and an iron so that every night she could wash and iron the blouse for the next day.

Unexpectedly, the design of the WAAC uniform had turned out to be a huge problem. Oveta knew it must look army-like but not be too masculine. Originally she approved a leather belt

Oveta Culp Hobby at a press conference in London, England, November 1942. *National Archives*

and pleated skirt—both too expensive, she was told. The designers initially chose two shades of blue. "No," Oveta insisted. "The uniform must be identical in color to the army and the design must also be similar." She decided against slacks and insisted on skirts and dresses to bolster the image of a feminine but competent soldier. She approved a hat design. It fit snugly and was nicknamed the "Hobby hat." (The rumor was that Oveta was the only one who looked good in it.) Finally, Pallas Athene would represent the WAAC. This Greek goddess was a perfect

---

WE'RE THE WOMEN OF THIS NATION

Some people trivialized the role of the women in the WAAC. For example, one magazine wrote, "Behavior was average young female. They put wet towels in each other's beds, tied knots in pajama legs."

While there *was* time for fun, these women—all volunteers—also understood they had a serious job to do. Oveta herself resolved to never smile when her photo was taken. She worked hard to maintain the professional image of the Corps. Once the United States entered the war, most women knew a family member, sweetheart, or friend who was involved. The war was real and so was the pride at being able to contribute. One of the first recruits, Ruby Jane Douglass, wrote a number of songs to honor the WAAC, echoing the sentiment most WAACs felt at the time.

We're the Women of this Nation
And Victory is our song
We will fight for preservation
Make our country strong
We will stand behind our Army
Our banner sky high will soar
We are known throughout the nation
Women's Army Auxiliary Corps!

symbol—she exemplified womanly virtues and was wise in issues of war and peace.

A training center was secured at Fort Des Moines, Iowa, and Oveta oversaw the officer candidates who arrived that July. The group selected had high credentials—many had college degrees and some even had advanced degrees. Almost all of them had been working prior to enlisting and so would bring valuable experience to the corps. A quarter of them were over 36 years old, mature enough to accomplish the demanding jobs.

But there were still many other problems. Because the WAAC was not technically part of the army, personnel often didn't authorize support. For example, Fort Des Moines was an old cavalry post, and the horse stables needed to be converted to barracks. Oveta asked army engineers for help. They refused; the WAAC was not part of the army and the army engineers did not have the authority to help them. She asked for army specialists to help develop a budget to present to Congress. The reaction was the same. Oveta and her team were forced to complete this task and others themselves, often staying up most of the night to get things done. Even transportation was a hassle. While all male officers had their own jeeps, Oveta had to call to the transportation pool for a car.

To top it all off, women did not receive the same benefits as men. Their pay was lower and they did not have the same rank. Out of the country, they were not entitled to overseas pay like the men were, or government life insurance and veteran's medical care. Until the "auxiliary" status was dropped a year later and the Corps became part of the Regular Army (now the WAC), Oveta found herself constantly tangled in red tape.

On July 12, 1945, Oveta was so exhausted that her health was in serious jeopardy. With problems at home—her husband, William, also had health issues—Oveta finally resigned from

Colonel Oveta Culp Hobby is sworn in as director of the Women's Army Corps (WAC), July 1943. *National Archives*

the WAC. She had been working at a breakneck speed for four years, but, oh, what the WAC had accomplished! At its highest strength, nearly 100,000 women served in the WAC. At the beginning, jobs for women were mostly in the baking, clerical, driving, or medical fields. Within one year, 406 jobs out of 628 military occupations were opened to qualifying women—a 400 percent increase. Most important, Oveta helped prove that women could and *would* continue to provide valuable contributions to the army. "We are earnestly determined to make this new chapter a serious contribution and not a feminine footnote," she said.

After resigning from the army and regaining her health, Oveta continued to work in public and private jobs. In 1952 she was appointed head of what soon became the Department of Health, Education, and Welfare. A serious, brilliant, and hard-working woman, she truly did carve a pathway for women to serve in leadership positions, particularly in the US Army. Oveta died at the age of 90 on August 16, 1995, in her home in Houston, Texas.

★ LEARN MORE ★

Oveta Culp Hobby: Colonel, Cabinet Member, Philanthropist by Debra L. Winegarten (Austin: University of Texas Press, 2014)

Women at War, a recruiting video produced by Warner Brothers Pictures in 1943. www.youtube.com/watch?v=ALow _k85n2s

Charity Adams Earley

Letters from Home

"While we don't anticipate that anything unusual will happen during your flight, the plane is equipped with emergency supplies to last you thirty days."

The officer doing the briefing went on to explain that the rubber emergency boats included sets of fishing gear. Charity Adams glanced at the other passengers. There were 19 of them, including Noel Campbell, a captain in the Women's Army Corps (WAC), who was going with her. Charity did not know where her assignment was, nor what exactly she would be doing there. What she did know was that today—January 26, 1945—the war in Europe needed people like her and Noel, and she was not about to ditch.

Charity followed the others to the C-54 cargo plane. Instead of the comfortable reclining seats she had hoped for, there were two rows of metal bucket seats facing each other inside the wide body of the plane. She buckled up, resisting the urge to open the sealed envelope in her pocket. Inside the envelope were the orders that would explain her mission. She had been directed not to look at them until at least an hour into the flight.

The engines roared to life and the propellers whirled, slowly at first and then faster and faster until they were an invisible blur. Charity braced herself as the plane took off. When an hour had elapsed, she opened the envelope.

This is to certify that, in accordance with so RESTRICTED ORDER, AGO, dated 20 JANUARY 1945, CHARITY E. ADAMS MAJ. L-500001 WAC, is ordered to proceed to BRITISH ISLES, USA, SOS LONDON, ENGLAND.

Britain! Major Charity Adams breathed out slowly. She was to be the commanding officer for the 6888th, a postal unit in charge of mail for the whole European Theater of Operations (ETO). She was also well aware that this was the only African American WAC unit serving overseas. It would be a daunting assignment. She worried about how she and the other women in the unit would be received in Europe. Then there was the mission itself. Millions of pieces of mail would need to be sorted, censored, and sent on to the intended recipients. Luckily, Charity was up to the task.

Charity Adams Earley was born in Columbia, South Carolina, on December 5, 1917. She was the oldest of four children. Her mother was a former schoolteacher and her father was a Methodist minister. Charity and her siblings referred to themselves as PKs, preacher's kids. She got used to the extra scrutiny from neighbors and members of her father's congregation. "My brother and I belonged to the great fraternity of PK's, preachers' kids, and we were not expected to behave like other children," she said. From an early age, Charity always worked hard to go above and beyond.

The 6888th Postal Battalion sorting the mail. *US Army Women's Museum, Fort Lee, Virginia*

One thing that Charity was not so good at was spelling. Another was singing. In college, the director of the music department told her "just work your mouth." Despite being a terrible singer, Charity was a terrific reader—and valedictorian of her high school class. Not only that, but she achieved a perfect attendance record in school. This led to a scholarship for college, and after earning a bachelor's degree in education from Wilberforce University in Ohio, Charity taught math and general science for four years. The job was steady, if not terribly challenging. Her life was set—but it was about to take a sudden turn.

In the spring of 1942, Charity received a letter and an invitation. As she read it, her heart started to hammer and she had to sit down. Suddenly, here was an alternative to the tedium of teaching year after year. The dean of women at Wilberforce University had recommended her for the newly formed Women's Army Auxiliary Corps (WAAC). Charity filled out the attached application and mailed it off just as the school year was coming to a close. However, when nothing happened immediately, she gave up on the army.

Charity was on her way to Ohio to take summer school graduate courses when her train made a brief, 15-minute stop in Knoxville, Tennessee. To her shock and amazement, her aunt

LAST HIRED, FIRST FIRED

US participation in World War II lasted from December 1941 until September 1945. At the time, there was deep racial tension in the United States. Not only was Charity forced to attend segregated schools—there were separate schools for African American and white children—but society attempted to keep the races apart in other ways as well. For example, signs for "Colored" and "White" people marked which entrances, stores, restrooms, water fountains, and service areas could be used by either race. Being black meant that you had to work twice as hard to prove yourself or get ahead. Prejudice and discrimination were rampant. While Charity needed a bachelor's degree to get her first teaching job, white teachers were hired with just a high school diploma. Additionally, pay and conditions were not equal—or fair. Laws gradually changed, but during World War II, an African American woman like Charity had two strikes against her: she was female and she was black.

was at the station looking for her. She found Charity in the "colored" section of the train, the seats set aside for African American passengers. "Call home immediately!" her aunt exclaimed.

Charity looked at the time. The train was due to leave in just a few minutes. There was no way she would be able to get in a long-distance call to her family before it left.

"Can you please hold the train while I make a phone call?" she asked the conductor.

"Sorry, I can't do that."

"Would you come with me then to make the call?"

The conductor paused, but then nodded his head. He followed Charity to the telephone booth. She was still fumbling with the operator to get the call to go through when the conductor looked at his watch and made a motion to leave. Charity grabbed his coattail and held on until she could finish the call.

It turned out that the army had finally gotten back to her. They had called her home and told her she was to report to Atlanta, Georgia, the following day at 8:00 AM. But Charity was on a train to Ohio! Impossible.

Her heart sank, but she did not give up. The army had called her back! There had to be a way to tell them she was still interested, even if she was going to miss the appointment.

Arriving in Columbus, Ohio, Charity went to the local army base at Fort Hayes. "I'm interested in joining the WAAC," she explained. "But I missed my first appointment." Finally, after being referred to person after person, someone was able—and willing—to help. She was granted an interview three days later. It did not take long to receive an acceptance letter. Charity reported to her swearing-in ceremony and prepared to leave for Des Moines, Iowa. She gathered everything on the army's list except for the suggested slacks and shorts—she did not wear either and she was not about to start now.

The day she took an oath to serve in the WAAC, the *Columbus Dispatch* newspaper ran pictures of the new recruits. Amazed, Charity later mused, "I, a Negro, had my picture on the front page of a white daily without having done anything criminal."

July 19, 1942, was a dark, rainy day. Charity stepped off the train and climbed into a large truck with several other women. Three miles later she was at Fort Des Moines.

"Will all the colored girls move over to this side."

THE WAAC—WHAT, WHERE, WHO?

"I do hereby establish a Women's Army Auxiliary Corps for non-combatant service with the Army of the United States for the purpose of further making available to the national defense the knowledge, skill, and special training of the women of this Nation."

President Franklin Roosevelt signed Executive Order 9163 on May 15, 1942. The order established the Women's Army Auxiliary Corps (WAAC), which, a year later, dropped its "auxiliary" status and became the WAC. The day after Roosevelt signed the order, the WAAC's first director, Oveta Culp Hobby, was sworn in. But where would this first contingent of recruits be trained? Director Hobby quickly chose Fort Des Moines and scrambled to get the old cavalry post ready in record time. The first recruits were 440 officer candidates, including 40 slots allocated for African Americans. Nicknamed the "ten percenters," the number of blacks was supposed to match the overall national population of African Americans.

Charity was stunned. She and the other women had just marched from the mess hall, where a host of reporters had snapped picture after picture while *all* the women, black and white, ate their first meal at the training center—*together*. Now they were in the reception center, where a young, red-haired officer was pointing to the separate area designated for the African American women. As progressive as the army was for opening its doors to women—at least in some capacity—it was still shamefully behind in integrating black and white soldiers. Charity had hoped for better. She unpacked her things in Quarters 54, the building set aside for the African American recruits. The separate housing was another harsh reminder of just how deep racial prejudices reached, even in the army. Perhaps Charity's position in the WAAC could help encourage change.

Charity excelled during the training, impressing those around her and proving her worth again and again. When

The 3rd Platoon, the first WAAC Officer Candidate School to graduate, Fort Des Moines, August 29, 1942. *US Army Women's Museum, Fort Lee, Virginia*

graduation day finally arrived on Saturday, August 29, 1942, it was a beautiful day. Outside, with several VIPs in attendance, Charity Adams was the first African American woman to be commissioned in the WAAC.

After the ceremony, Charity moved from the training barracks into a house on officer's row—unfortunately still segregated. An officer now, she would be in charge of training other African American troops. It was a great responsibility and Charity dove right in, again excelling at this position of leadership. Of her time there, she remarked, "We worked hard at making soldiers out of civilians."

She knew she was making a difference.

In December 1944 Charity was called into the office of the commandant, Colonel Frank U. McCoskrie—a man the women nicknamed Colonel Mac. "How would you like to go overseas?" he asked her.

Charity, now Major Charity Adams, was not sure. She had accomplished so much at Fort Des Moines and had thought she would continue her work there forever. However, she knew that other WACs had already been assigned overseas, though no African American units. This opportunity was something new and challenging, and Charity could not help feeling a thrill of excitement. She told Colonel Mac that she would go wherever she was ordered.

In late January 1945 the plane Charity was flying on landed at Prestwick, Scotland. From there Charity took another plane to London; the next day, after a breakfast of powdered eggs and soybean sausage—but with real toast, thankfully—Charity and Captain Noel Campbell, her executive officer and second in command, traveled to Birmingham. Charity would be the commanding officer of the postal directory service there. The 6888th was stationed at the King Edward School, an old steam-heated building with outdoor showers. The officers' quarters were in two houses across the street. When the rest of the troops arrived by ship, their job would be to sort and redirect mail to approximately seven million service members in the European Theater of Operations. When Charity saw the masses of letters

SIX TRIPLE EIGHT

"No mail, low morale." This was the motto of the battalion of African American women who made up the 6888th Central Postal Directory. The 6888th Battalion arrived by ship in two contingents in February and March 1945. Immediately, officers organized the women into five companies. Headquarters was in charge of administration and services, and Companies A, B, C, and D focused on dealing with the incredible buildup of mail, including six airplane hangars full of Christmas packages. Some of these contained food items, so there were mice and rats to contend with as well. Adding to the difficulty of proper delivery, packages were sometimes labeled vaguely: "Buster, U.S. Army" or "Junior, U.S. Army." Even when mail was properly addressed, units moved frequently, and it was challenging to find out where to redirect the letters and packages. There were 31 officers and nearly 900 enlisted WACs to accomplish the task of clearing this backlog of mail. The "Six Triple Eight" worked around the clock, organized into three eight-hour shifts. Every shift handled an average of 65,000 pieces of mail. Their orders were to accomplish this in six months. The 6888th finished in three.

Major Charity Adams stands next to Lieutenant General John C. H. Lee as he reviews her troops, Birmingham, England, February 15, 1945. Captain Abbie Noel Campbell stands next to the podium. *Gladys (Anderson) Thomas Collection, Women's Memorial Foundation Collection*

and packages stacked up from a two-year backlog, it was hard not to feel overwhelmed.

Working nonstop, the 6888th cleared out the buildup of mail in Birmingham. In fact, they had just gotten comfortable when Charity received new orders: the unit would be heading to France. There was another enormous pileup of mail waiting for them there, and by now, this WAC battalion had proven that they could handle it. Plus, with the war's end in sight, the army wanted the postal service closer to where service members could receive their mail. Charity made plans to move everyone to Rouen, France, taking several trips herself across the English Channel to set things up.

On May 7, 1945, Charity left once more for France and arrived in Paris on May 8, on her way to Rouen. On a train through the

The 6888th Postal Battalion in Rouen, France, 1945. *US Army Women's Museum, Fort Lee, Virginia*

French countryside, Charity wondered at the great number of people at each of the train stations. Once in Paris, there were even larger crowds, jubilant and celebrating. It finally dawned on Charity: it was Victory in Europe Day—V-E Day! The war was over here, and the French were ecstatic with victory. As she made her way to the hotel she would be staying in that evening, people asked for—or simply took—bits of her uniform for a souvenir, including her cap, insignia, and the braid on her sleeves. When someone took a shoestring, Charity decided to stay indoors that evening. The boisterous celebration continued.

After victory was announced and the 6888th WACs were stationed in Rouen, it seemed to Charity as if every Allied man on the continent came to see the women working there. Some were brothers, husbands, fiancés, or boyfriends, but others—many, many others—were just interested in seeing American women after being so long away from their homes in the States. At first it was fun to have all that attention, but after a while, representatives from the five companies met with Charity about the problem. The men were around too much! There was no

VICTORY IN EUROPE DAY

During World War II, two main groups fought against each other. The Allied forces included Great Britain, the Soviet Union, France, and the United States. The Axis forces were Germany, Italy, and Japan.

After the invasion of Normandy—D-day—Allied powers liberated France from its German occupiers. Adolf Hitler, the dictator of Germany, ordered a counterattack that became known as the Battle of the Bulge. Germany lost this conflict as well. Finally, the last major battle of the war was the Battle of Berlin—it took place from April 16 until May 2, 1945. Hitler committed suicide inside a bunker in this city on April 30 when it was clear that Germany would lose the war.

On May 7, the new German commander, General Alfred Jodl, traveled to Reims, France. There, in a redbrick schoolhouse that Supreme Allied Commander Dwight D. Eisenhower was using for his headquarters, Germany signed an unconditional surrender to the war. The next day was declared V-E Day, and people celebrated the end of the war in Europe. World War II was not quite over, though; war still raged against Japan in the Pacific.

privacy for the women to do chores like personal laundry or washing their hair.

Charity had an idea: No men Mondays.

Once a week, no men, except those on official business (plus the German prisoners of war who had been assigned to work for the 6888th and their guards) would be allowed on the post. Mostly these men were just curious, but some were overly insistent that they be let on base. Charity asked that the WAC military police—MPs—stationed at the gate be allowed to carry firearms in case things got out of hand. This request was denied. Instead, a British officer who Charity knew offered to teach the women the martial art jiu-jitsu. Problem solved!

Charity still had her own problem with the intrusive hordes of men. Many officers were insisting that they come and see the commander on "urgent" business or in order to "inspect" the unit. Taking time for these visits was causing Charity to fall behind in her work, until she thought of a solution for this issue as well. She had a quarter-inch cut from the front two legs of the chair in front of her desk. It made it very difficult for anyone to sit for a long time. Suddenly the visits were brief!

Charity stayed in France until December 1945 when the last of the 6888th service members were shipped back to the States. They had cleared out the enormous buildup of mail in Rouen and then had moved to Paris to continue their work. Finally, it was time to go home. Charity boarded a troop transport ship this time instead of a plane. The ship was a re-outfitted German luxury yacht with over 100 times the number of people aboard than what it had been designed for. In yet another show of prejudice, a unit of white WAC nurses refused to sail with Charity in command, even though she was the highest-ranking officer. The ship sailed without the nurses. Twelve days later, it arrived in New York City.

Home at last! Shortly after arriving in the States, Charity was promoted to lieutenant colonel, the highest military rank for a female aside from the WAC director. She retired from the army on March 26, 1946, to earn the master's degree she had started before the war. She worked at various jobs including one at the Veterans Administration and another managing a music school—a challenge with her lack of musical talent. Then Charity got married, and she focused on raising a family and helping her community. In an America that still harbored racism and discrimination, she worked for positive change. In her own words, "I have opened a few doors, broken a few barriers, and, I hope, smoothed the way to some degree for the next generation." On January 13, 2002, Charity died at the age of 83 in Dayton, Ohio.

Charity Adams Earley and the 6888th Postal Battalion. *US Army Women's Museum, Fort Lee, Virginia*

★ LEARN MORE ★

The National WWII Museum, New Orleans, www.nationalww2
   museum.org

One Woman's Army: A Black Officer Remembers the WAC by Charity
   Adams Earley (College Station: Texas A&M University Press,
   1989)

*To Serve My Country, to Serve My Race: The Story of the Only Afri-
   can American WACs Stationed Overseas During World War II* by
   Brenda L. Moore (New York: New York University Press,
   1996)

Margaret KC Yang

Pearl of Oʻahu

W AR! OAHU BOMBED BY JAPANESE PLANES
The black letters took up half the front page of the *Honolulu Star-Bulletin*'s first Extra. By afternoon on December 7, 1941, the black smoke from burning buildings and planes took up half the sky over Oʻahu, Hawaiʻi.

Seventeen-year-old Margaret Kyung Choon Yang still could not believe it. Had it been only this morning that she was lazing in bed for a few extra minutes (because it was Sunday)? Had it been just hours ago when she had first heard the roar of airplanes, thinking it was simply another US military maneuver? After all, with six military airfields dotting the island—and Wheeler Field practically next door—there were training exercises all the time.

It was not until she had gone outside and squinted into the sun that she saw the red circles painted on the wings and bodies of the airplanes. These were not American planes—they were

Japanese! And there were more and more and more of them.
As the planes whined overhead, Margaret suddenly understood
the dull thuds she was also hearing: the island was under attack!
The noise was from the detonation of bombs. Now she noticed
the puffs of smoke from American antiaircraft guns too. But it
was not enough. In moments, buildings and planes at Wheeler
Field were obliterated, flames out of control and smoke billow-
ing into the brilliant sky. Shocking and terrifying, war had come
to Margaret's island home.

The rest of the day was a blur. She listened as special
announcements played constantly from Honolulu's radio station KGU: "Citizens are urged to remain calm and avoid unnec-
essary confusion due to hysteria."

At one point there was an explosion nearby. An enemy
plane had crashed into a home right in Wahiawa! Was anybody
hurt? Would more planes follow? And what about the rest of
the island—how many were getting hurt—*killed*—from all of
this bombing? Margaret closed her eyes. What was next? Would
Japanese troops launch a land attack to finish the job?

Margaret, normally so practical and efficient, felt a spidery
fear creeping up the back of her neck.

By later that Sunday, Hawai'i was operating under martial
law. At 6:00 PM Margaret helped turn out all lights for a mandatory blackout. At 6:04 there was another radio announcement:
"From now on nobody allowed out of their homes." All night
Margaret huddled in the dark with her brothers and sisters.
Through that sleepless night, rumors flew as thick as the bombs
had earlier that day: *The enemy was parachuting onto the island.
The water supply had been poisoned. Japanese spies were sabotaging
vital facilities . . .*

Margaret had no idea which, if any, of the rumors were true.
However, she did know that, in the space of 24 hours, life had

JAPAN ATTACKS!

"Wave after wave of bombers streamed through the clouded morning sky from the southwest and flung their missiles on a city resting in peaceful Sabbath calm," the *Honolulu Star-Bulletin* reported.

For the residents of O'ahu, Hawai'i, the Japanese attack on December 7, 1941, was a complete surprise. Expecting a contingent of American planes from the mainland, the officer in charge did not immediately recognize the danger when radar picked up a large number of planes flying in. However, in just under two hours, approximately 2,400 people had been killed, including 49 civilians. Nearly 1,200 were wounded. The attack completely destroyed three battleships and over 150 aircraft. Scores of other ships, aircraft, and buildings were severely damaged. A battleship, the USS *Arizona*, was hit by a 1,760-pound bomb. With 1.5 million gallons of oil aboard, the wreck burned for over two and a half days. Even today, oil continues to leak from the ruined hull, still visible in the shallow waters of Pearl Harbor.

The day after the attack, on December 8, 1941, the United States declared war on Japan.

turned upside down for her family and the rest of the people living in Hawai'i.

School was canceled until further notice. Instead, the school building was being used to house surviving soldiers whose barracks had been bombed.

No private cars were allowed on the highways.

All personal photos and motion pictures of the attack were to be turned over to the military immediately.

Beaches were lined with barbed wire and guards were assigned to patrol them.

All mail leaving the island now had to be censored.

(((((((((((((((((((((((((((((((((★)))))))))))))))))))))))))))))))))))))

JAPANESE AMERICANS UNDER THE MICROSCOPE

On February 19, 1942, President Franklin Roosevelt signed Executive Order 9066 with unanimous support from Congress. The order declared sections of the West Coast—California, Oregon, and Washington—to be military zones. Over 110,000 mainland Japanese Americans were ordered to leave their homes, along with another 2,000 from Hawai'i. Entire families were forcibly removed and sent to "relocation centers" (internment camps) for the remainder of the war.

These detention centers had barbed wire fences and guards, even though 70 percent of the people inside were American citizens and most had never been accused of any crime. A small number of people of German and Italian descent were also sent to the camps. World War II eventually ended, and the last camp was closed in March 1946. Years later a government-appointed committee published a study called *Personal Justice Denied*. The study showed that the vast majority of the Japanese interned were loyal to the United States. However, it was not until nearly 50 years later that the US government apologized for the treatment of the people forced into these camps.

(((((((((((((((((((((((((((((((((★)))))))))))))))))))))))))))))))))))))

Margaret learned that even buying food was temporarily forbidden until an inventory could be made. It made sense. With crops of mostly pineapples and sugar, Hawaiʻi depended on outside imports for nearly everything else. And right now, enemy submarines—loaded with torpedoes—patrolled the waters off Hawaiʻi's coast. Margaret wondered how long it would be before commercial ships could get through.

Maybe the worst thing was the talk about all the people of Japanese ancestry who lived on the islands. Margaret's family was originally from Korea, but plenty of Margaret's friends were Japanese. Many of them had lived in the United States their whole lives. Still, fear and doubt buzzed around Margaret's hometown of Wahiawa. Were the Japanese on the island spies? Would these people turn on their friends and neighbors and side with the United States' enemy, Japan? There was talk that these people would be taken away to camps. Margaret trusted her friends, but she was not the one making the decisions.

Margaret KC Yang was born on July 21, 1924, in Kunia, on the island of Oʻahu in Hawaiʻi. She was smack in the middle of 12 siblings and the second-oldest daughter. Both her parents had immigrated from Korea, her father to work for the Hawaiʻian Plantation Company and her mother to join her family, who were already in Hawaiʻi. Margaret's parents were married in 1912. Years later, her father moved the family to Wahiawa when he took a job as a carpenter at Wheeler Field. It was three years before the attack on Pearl Harbor.

Margaret's family was close. She loved when her father played his bamboo flute, and she appreciated her mother, a dutiful, hardworking woman who cared deeply for all her children. The attack on Pearl Harbor made life a lot busier. With the announcement of American involvement in World War II, her father started working 12-hour shifts. Margaret helped at home

Margaret KC Yang grew up on the island of Oʻahu. *Jama Rattigan*

in any way she could, including organizing the rest of her siblings. No problem! Margaret was good at that—organizing and
being responsible.

In December 1941 Margaret was a senior in high school.
Although schools reopened the following February, her class
did not have a prom or commencement exercises because of the
war. Instead, Margaret and her classmates walked everywhere
carrying gas masks and helping with the war effort. Some of
Margaret's friends filled out the registration cards mandatory

for every resident on Oʻahu. Others helped with the fingerprint-
ing that went along with this registration. Margaret worked as
a junior hostess at the United Service Organization (USO), a
club for military service members and their families. Everyone
waited for what was going to come next. Margaret knew what
would come next for her: the moment recruitment was opened
in Hawaiʻi, Margaret aimed to join the Women's Army Corps
(WAC).

In October 1944 the WAC finally set up recruitment offices
in Hawaiʻi, though women from the mainland had been eligible to enlist since 1942. Margaret's parents were appalled at the
idea of her being in the army. It wasn't "a respectable thing to
do," her mother exclaimed, even though several of her brothers
were already serving. However, Margaret was determined, and
after much pleading and much convincing, her parents finally
relented. Margaret hurried to the recruitment office to register.

On December 18, 1944, Margaret received instructions to
report to the Territorial Guard Armory to be outfitted in a WAC
uniform. She arrived promptly at 8:15 AM. The woolen uniform
was heavy and terribly hot. The stockings felt odd against her
normally bare legs. It was hard for Margaret to imagine a place
where she would need such warm clothes. She had to admit,
though, the uniform was stylish. With her garrison hat to complete the look, Margaret felt like a real soldier.

Her orders came shortly after Christmas. They read, "The
following named enlisted women/ERC are recalled to Active
Duty and will report to the CO Casual WAC Detachment, Territorial Guard Armory, South Hotel and Miller Sts., Honolulu,
T. H. [Territory of Hawaiʻi] by 1100 27 December 1944." The
list included 62 women. Written boldly beside Margaret's name
was her service number, A-50-037. She was one of the youngest
recruits.

Margaret and her younger brother Joe. *Jama Rattigan*

Margaret was 20 years old when she said goodbye to her family and boarded the SS *Matsonia*, a former tourist ship now converted to transport troops. A mixture of emotions pulsed through her as she stood on the deck: anticipation, uncertainty—and determination. She had never even been off the island, and now, imagine, she was sailing all the way to California!

After docking in San Francisco, Margaret followed the others to the train station. She traveled by train—another first—through New Mexico, Arizona, Texas, Arkansas, Tennessee . . . In Amarillo, Texas, Margaret saw her first snow and understood the need for the heavy woolen uniform.

Basic training was located at Fort Oglethorpe, Georgia. The course was serious and intense, but the camaraderie drew Margaret closer to the other women. Her days started at 5:30 AM when she dressed quickly and made sure her bed was in order—inspections required that it be "just so."

On the double! Run! She marched with the rest of the WACs to reveille at 6:00 AM. They stood in formation saluting the flag while the bugle played its famous tune. Next, she was marching to breakfast in the mess hall, where she lined up cafeteria-style. Then it was marching to the rigorous schedule of classes: army organization, map reading, first aid, personal hygiene, and what to do in an air or chemical attack. Then drills and . . . more marching. Saturday evening was their time to unwind.

During basic training Margaret witnessed something nearly as shocking as the day her beloved Oʻahu had been bombed. This was the segregation of black people and white people. One day when Margaret got on a city bus with some of the other WACs, they made their way to seats at the back.

"Up front!" the bus driver admonished them. Margaret glanced at the sign defining the seating areas. Apparently, Asian Americans were lumped together with the white passengers. Margaret reluctantly moved to the front. The next time she was on the bus, she ignored the sign again.

"You can't sit back there, miss." This happened several times. And it was not just on the bus. There were signs in restaurants and restrooms too. Black customers were to go one way, white customers the other. Margaret got used to the scolding, though she did not get used to the discrimination. *Isn't there something more important to worry about?* she thought. *Isn't there a war going on?*

Margaret received orders for her first assignment. After training at the army's clerical school at Fort Des Moines, Iowa, she was stationed at Camp Stoneman, California. Her job was to process orders for overseas troop movement. She worked hard, her natural ability to organize a real asset on the job.

Corporal Margaret KC Yang was one of the first 60 women from Hawai'i who enlisted in the WAC during World War II. *Margaret (Yang) Kim Collection, Women's Memorial Foundation Collection*

Suddenly all Margaret's anxious waiting was over. It was V-J Day, Victory over Japan Day. Japan had surrendered at last, putting an end to World War II. Everywhere, people were ecstatic, and Margaret was too. She joined in a local victory march. Now a corporal, she received an honorable discharge on June 27, 1946. Before this, however, she spent a few more months working for the army, both back in Oʻahu and on the mainland. One day she was walking to a friend's house when she caught a handsome young man staring at her, obviously impressed to see such an attractive young lady in uniform. When they ran into each other again—this time when Margaret was driving her brother's jeep—there was no turning back. That man became her husband two years later.

Margaret spent the rest of her life working and raising a family on Oʻahu. After a full and active life, she died at the age of 89 on April 9, 2014. She was buried with full military honors, likely the last remaining member of the first company of WACs from Hawaiʻi.

Margaret's time in the army may have been relatively short, but she never forgot it. One of her most treasured possessions was the letter signed by President Harry Truman:

"To you who answered the call of your country and served in its Armed Forces to bring about the total defeat of the enemy, I extend heartfelt thanks of a grateful nation."

Today, standing at the foot of Oʻahu's majestic mountains, it is almost as if you can hear the song composed by one of Hawaiʻi's original brave WAC women:

> *W-A-C, W-A-C, Women's Army Corps.*
> *We were the first ones, we were the first ones.*
> *From Hawaiʻi nei.*
> *Every nationality, every nationality*

You can think of.
H-A-W, H-A-W, A-Double I
Hawai'i, Hawai'i, We're the girls from Hawai'i.
Hawai'i, Hawai'i, please wait for me.

 ⭐ LEARN MORE ⭐

National Park Service, World War II Valor in the Pacific National
  Monument, www.nps.gov/valr/faqs.htm
United States Army Museum of Hawai'i, www.hiarmymuseum
  soc.org/index.html

PART III

Global Conflict

The Late 20th Century

★ ★ ★ ★ ★

A t the close of World War II, women had proven that they could—and did—offer valuable contributions to the army. There was no question that their input had positively influenced the outcome of the war. By Victory in Europe Day, May 8, 1945, over 140,000 women had served in the Women's Army Corps (WAC). Yet when the war ended, the future of the WAC was in jeopardy. The training centers at Fort Oglethorpe and Fort Des Moines closed, and some people thought that women's participation in the army was over. Others argued that progress could not turn backward—the army still needed women for postwar occupations as well as for future national emergencies. The debate continued, but WAC strength dwindled to a few thousand women.

Finally, on June 12, 1948, President Harry Truman signed a new law. The Women's Armed Services Integration Act of 1948 stated that women were now a permanent component of the Regular Army and the Reserve Army Corps. Officials established a training center at Fort Lee, Virginia. However, there were still stipulations that separated the WAC from the rest

99

of the army. There was a restriction on the number of women allowed to enlist. Women could not rise above the rank of lieutenant colonel—except in the one position of WAC director, who was a colonel. Also, female officers could only command other women, not men. Just as demoralizing, the conditions at Fort Lee were terrible—the barracks were little more than flimsy shacks and hardly encouraged other women to enlist.

The Korean War began on June 25, 1950, when North Korea invaded South Korea. The United Nations, including the United States and Great Britain, supported South Korea. China and the Soviet Union supported the communist government of North Korea. Suddenly, the United States was at war again and women were needed to step into army roles. WAC reservists—both volunteer and not—were mobilized to serve in Japan, across the Sea of Japan from Korea. A few women served in administrative positions in South Korea as well. In 1953, with little resolved, the United States signed a truce to end the conflict.

Back in the States, there was no doubt that women would continue to serve permanently in the WAC. A new training facility at Fort McClellan, Alabama, opened in 1954. For the next two decades, Fort McClellan became the home of the WAC Center and School. Thousands of recruits passed through this training facility until the army disestablished the WAC in 1977. The women trained there went on to serve all over the world. In the next major conflict, the Vietnam War, a detachment of approximately 90 women were stationed outside of Saigon. A new batch of WACs rotated in each year from 1967 to 1972. Additionally, a smaller unit of WACs worked directly for Commanding General William Westmoreland at his headquarters in Saigon.

Since women were already excelling in challenging and often dangerous positions of tremendous responsibility, it was

Elizabeth P. Hoisington is promoted to brigadier general. *US Army Women's Museum, Fort Lee, Virginia*

obvious that they deserved equal treatment to that of their male counterparts performing similar tasks. On November 8, 1967, Congress lifted the rank restrictions for women. Now qualified women could potentially earn the rank they deserved, all the way up to general officer. Other constraints were lifted as well, and there followed a number of army "firsts."

On June 11, 1970, Elizabeth Hoisington, one of the WAC's original recruits, was one of two first-ever female officers promoted to brigadier general. Next, the army's premier service academy at West Point opened to women in 1976 with the initial coed class graduating in 1980. By the early 1990s, 80 percent of military positions were open to men *and* women. In Operation Desert Shield and Desert Storm (1990–1991), women served by transporting soldiers and supplies, driving and repairing heavy vehicles, launching missiles, guarding prisoners of war,

commanding various units, and other crucial duties. Stateside, women served in multiple positions of authority too. On
the cusp of the 21st century, Celia Adolphi earned the rank of
major general in 1999, the first female in the Army Reserve to
achieve this honor. Women proved indispensable to the army.
Never again would the United States engage in a major conflict
without the inclusion of both men and women serving in key
military positions.

Elizabeth P. Hoisington

Good Old Army

Elizabeth Hoisington was sick with worry when she heard that German forces had captured her younger brother Bob. It was the spring of 1945 and Elizabeth was serving in the Women's Army Corp (WAC) in Paris. She knew that Corporal Bob Hoisington was a tank gunner for Company D, 23rd Tank Battalion. She learned that on March 19, 1945, his company was patrolling near Ludwigshafen, on the west bank of the Rhine River in Germany, when German soldiers took him prisoner. As soon as she could, Elizabeth set out to find him.

V-E Day—Victory in Europe—was only weeks away when Bob's Sherman tank came under fire. An artillery shell hit the vehicle, and the blast threw Bob from the tank commander's hatch. He landed, wounded, on cold, hard ground. His first thought was of his winter clothes, destroyed along with the rest of the tank. Next he had a more positive realization: he was still alive.

A German soldier nudged Bob with a gun. Shivering, he stood up as it began to snow and sleet. The enemy officer handed him a Russian greatcoat and Bob started marching. That was as far as the generosity went. Along with several others, Bob spent 41 days as a prisoner of war (POW) at Stalag VII-A in southern Germany.

Meanwhile, Elizabeth had been in France since July 14, 1944, just over a month after Allied forces landed at Normandy for the D-day invasion. In late August she was one of six army women who arrived in Paris five days after Allies liberated the city. As executive officer, Elizabeth's job was to help set up a WAC detachment in the city. When she heard that her brother had been captured, she knew she needed to find him.

Elizabeth loaded chocolate bars and cigarettes into a jeep. In May 1945 Europe was in turmoil, and these were the surest currency to pay for things she might need along the way. Knowing that Bob had been set free, but not knowing what condition he was in, Elizabeth traveled nearly 400 miles to find him. When she did locate him near the newly liberated prisoner-of-war camp, he was considerably thinner than she remembered.

To survive, he had eaten potatoes and sawdust bread. Indeed, the food situation had gotten desperate. Elizabeth related later that he "vividly remembers killing and eating a cat."

Elizabeth was just thankful Bob was alive and that he would soon go home. She sent notification to her parents back in the States, and after a brief and grateful visit, she went back to Paris to work.

Elizabeth Paschel Hoisington was born on November 3, 1918, in Newton, Kansas. Her high school yearbook called her "a true supporter of good old Army." Her classmates from the College of Notre Dame of Maryland said she was "always Army all the way." Indeed, Elizabeth lived and breathed army her whole life.

D-DAY

D-day, also known as the Battle of Normandy, signified a major turning point in World War II. It took place on June 6, 1944. At 6:30 AM, the largest seaborne attack in history began on the coast of France. The massive undertaking involved:

>> over 150,000 American, Canadian, and British troops

>> nearly 6,000 ships and landing craft

>> 50 miles of heavily fortified coastline

And at Omaha Beach, the worst area of fighting, soldiers had to cross 200 yards of exposed beach before they could take cover.

D-day changed the course of the war. Despite 4,413 recorded Allied deaths on that day alone, the Allied troops were victorious in breaking through the German defenses and pushing through to the rest of France. They liberated Paris 81 days later. However, it was another year before Germany officially and unconditionally surrendered. Today a 172.5-acre American cemetery overlooks Omaha Beach and the English Channel. Over 9,000 American military personnel are buried there, including 41 sets of brothers and 3 American women.

At her promotion ceremony to director of the WAC, Elizabeth's brother told a newspaper reporter, "All she had to hear was the fife and drum and she was ready to go."

The daughter of an army officer, Elizabeth moved 14 times with her family to various army posts: New Jersey, the Philippines, Georgia, New York, Ohio, Washington State, Mississippi, California, and twice each to Kansas, Alaska, and Maryland. From a family of six children, all her brothers attended West Point Military Academy and served as army officers. Bob, the brother who had been a POW, entered the academy when he got back from Europe. Even her two sisters married officers. Elizabeth understood and loved the army from an early age. As a young girl, she had her older brother Perry's West Point overcoat cut down to fit her smaller size. It was a crushing blow that, as a female, Elizabeth could not enlist herself.

When Elizabeth was 18, laws prevented women from serving in the army. Since she could not enlist, she went off to college to earn a degree in chemistry with a minor in math. She already knew how to ride horses and shoot a rifle—her father had taught her both growing up. At college she played several sports and added to her growing collection of tennis trophies. She did not know it at the time, but she was preparing for a long and successful army career. She gained valuable leadership experience when she taught riding and tennis at a girls' summer camp in Pennsylvania. She developed a keen attention to detail with her studies and in housekeeping; her side of the dorm room was meticulously neat and organized. One thing she did not excel at in college—or ever—was the ability to type. Elizabeth was a hunt-and-peck typist her entire life. Years later, her sister joked, "She said if she had learned to type, she would never have been promoted to general." She meant that if Elizabeth had been a good typist, she would have been recruited as a clerk instead of for various leadership positions.

Elizabeth had just graduated from college when President Roosevelt signed into law the Women's Army Auxiliary Corps

(WAAC), establishing an opportunity for women to serve in the army. As soon as a recruiter came around, Elizabeth rushed to enlist, after first convincing her mother and grandmothers that it would be OK. (Elizabeth's father helped to persuade them.) She was sworn in on October 22, 1942, in Seattle, Washington, and came home with service number A-909193 and a new sense

《《《《《《《《《《《《《《《《《《《《《《《《《《《《 ★ 》》》》》》》》》》》》》》》》》》》》》》》》》》》》》

WAAC TO WAC

Canada and Britain already had well-established female army branches by the time the United States opened certain army jobs to women. After much debate, the US Congress passed a bill on May 14, 1942, that allowed for a Women's Army Auxiliary Corps (WAAC). Pallas Athene, Greek goddess of victory and womanly virtue, was chosen to represent this new initiative. A director was appointed, and the corps was up and running. Immediately, issues involving uniforms, a training center, and recruitment cropped up. The problem was that the WAAC was working *with* the army versus *in* the army. Anytime the director wanted to get anything done, red tape bogged down her decisions. Who was responsible for paying for necessities? Who could authorize any decisions or expenditures? Plus, as an auxiliary corps, the women in the WAAC did not receive the same benefits as the men.

On July 1, 1943, the auxiliary status of the WAAC was dropped and it became the Women's Army Corps (WAC) with pay and privileges equal to its male counterparts. By the end of the war, nearly 100,000 women served, including approximately 17,000 who served overseas.

《《《《《《《《《《《《《《《《《《《《《《《《《《《《 ★ 》》》》》》》》》》》》》》》》》》》》》》》》》》》》》

of purpose. Soon after, she graduated from basic training as Auxiliary Elizabeth Hoisington (a rank equivalent to private). Next she headed to Fort Des Moines, Iowa, to attend WAAC Officer Candidate School Class #27, starting on March 30, 1943.

Now an officer, Elizabeth got to work.

A year after graduating from the WAAC, Elizabeth received orders to sail to London on D-day +38, the 38th day after Allied forces had launched the invasion in Normandy, France. Elizabeth packed her helmet and other gear and boarded a cruiser for France. The ship was packed: troops and a small contingent of WACs—49 enlisted women and 5 officers, including Elizabeth—crowded aboard.

"WAC personnel prepare to disembark," the ship's loudspeaker blared. Elizabeth stepped carefully down the ladder onto the LCI (landing craft infantry). Once ashore, she could not help pausing to stare around her. Just weeks before, this area had been the scene of one of the bloodiest battles of the war. She took in the blackened skeletons of former vehicles and the remains of cement bunkers where Germans had picked off the soldiers who first came ashore. A hasty graveyard of silent crosses rested nearby. Soon she and the others were jolting along a road pockmarked with shell craters. They passed through the countryside where French villagers paused in their efforts to clear away wreckage to wave at the women. Elizabeth waved back.

For the next weeks, Elizabeth lived in tents. Outside Valognes, men dug ditches around these tents as the skies poured with rain for eight straight days. Elizabeth and the others survived on army K and C rations—individually boxed meals—and treated water that was sometimes in short supply. The water came from large Lister bags, canvas containers with added chlorine to make it safe for drinking. When there was only one helmet-ful extra, the women first brushed their teeth, then did a quick body and hair wash. If there was any water left, they rinsed their clothes.

When Paris was liberated about a month after the WACs landed at Normandy, Elizabeth and five others formed an advance detachment and entered the city. Elizabeth's job was to help set things up for the thousands of WACs who would be following shortly. They took over offices near the Arc de Triomphe where Germans had been working just days before. Service for power and light was still unreliable, and food supplies were scarce. The women had a strict curfew of 8:00 PM. If anyone had to work later, an armed soldier escorted her to her room. Once again, Elizabeth proved her ability to organize. For her efficient and swift work to get things ready for the incoming WACs, Brigadier General Allen R. Kimball awarded Elizabeth a Bronze Star, a prestigious military honor. Her citation read:

For meritorious service in connection with military operations as a Detachment officer . . . Lieutenant Hoisington upon the movement of the headquarters from Valognes, France, to Paris, was charged with the difficult task of quartering, accommodating, and orienting all the Women's Army Corps personnel. By attention to duty and untiring effort, all the arrangements were completed for this difficult task, and all the details were carried out with great efficiency. Her devotion to duty and exceptional ability are an outstanding example of leadership reflecting great credit for herself and the United States Army.

The French government expressed their gratitude as well. They awarded Elizabeth the Croix de Guerre (war cross) with Silver Star.

Brigadier General Kimball pins Bronze Star on Lieutenant Hoising-ton, 1944. *US Army Women's Museum, Fort Lee, Virginia*

Despite victory in Europe, the conflict with Japan continued in the Pacific Theater. Finally, Japan formally surrendered on September 2, 1945. Elizabeth found herself in the heat of the action once again. She spent two years from 1948 to 1950 serving in Tokyo. American troops under General Douglas MacArthur occupied the country until 1952.

Elizabeth went back to the States in 1950, where her career continued to soar. Repeating the frequent travels of her childhood, from the time she returned from Japan until she took over as director of the Women's Army Corps, Elizabeth held 10 different positions with as many moves, including another three-year stint in Paris. Then, at an August 1, 1966, ceremony, Elizabeth was promoted to both colonel *and* director of the WAC. She arrived in her new office at the Pentagon every morning at 7:45.

By now she had 11 medals, a small apartment three minutes from her work, and a Cadillac that she fiercely protected from anyone with muddy shoes.

WORLD WAR II: WHAT'S TO EAT?

World War II troops in the field had no mess hall (kitchen) available, so they survived on C and K rations—daily combat food rations. The rations were individual boxed meals, one for breakfast, supper (lunch), and dinner. C rations included food packaged in cans to preserve its quality and longevity. K rations were a lighter (in weight) version, initially created for paratroopers who could not transport heavy cans of food. Along with the boxed meal was an accessory pack that included toilet paper, water purification tablets, chewing gum, a can opener, and cigarettes with matches.

Then there was US Field Ration D. Before American involvement in the war, the army approached the Hershey Chocolate Company. Captain Paul Logan was in charge of negotiations. He directed the company to create a chocolate bar that weighed 4 ounces, was high in energy, and could withstand high temperatures. Captain Logan also instructed that the bar "taste just a little better than a boiled potato." The army wanted the bar as an emergency energy source only. If it was too tasty, they reasoned that soldiers might be tempted to eat it immediately. The resulting 600-calorie bar, made with oat flour, was edible, but not tasty. And there was no danger of it melting—it was so hard that service members had to shave off slivers with a knife.

Captain Hoisington (right) with WAC director Colonel Hallaren, Japan, 1950. *US Army Women's Museum, Fort Lee, Virginia*

In her new job as director, Elizabeth was in charge of over 10,000 WACs. At the time of her appointment, women worked in 180 out of a possible 450 army jobs, though rank advancement was limited. There were 49 WAC units across the country and 16 overseas, including a detachment in Vietnam. (Elizabeth traveled there to inspect them and boost morale in September 1967.) During her tenure as director, she worked to increase WAC recruitment, and numbers swelled to nearly 13,000. She helped expand officer promotions and opportunities. Working to add more career fields for women, Elizabeth helped open jobs in intelligence, electronics, personnel administration, and air traffic control. It is no wonder that shortly after her appointment, an article in the *Sun* magazine predicted, "Colonel Hoisington may yet catch up with highest-ranking brother Perry—Major General Perry M. Hoisington, USAF, Ret. (retired). An equal opportunity bill to remove grade limitations for female officers has just left the House Armed Services Committee."

Elizabeth never, *ever* imagined she would rise to the rank of brigadier general. However, at a ceremony held on June 11, 1970, Elizabeth P. Hoisington was one of the first two women simultaneously promoted to this status. Wearing her new general's insignia, she tucked her father's colonel's eagles in her pocket and touched the Pallas Athene pin on her lapel. Pallas Athene, she reminded the audience, was the symbol for the WAC. She added, her voice confident and poised, "Pallas Athene is shining brighter today than she has in her history."

Elizabeth worked one more year as director of the WAC before she retired in 1971 after serving nearly three decades in the army. She continued to serve her community as a frequent public speaker and a member of a number of boards. She died on

Director Colonel Elizabeth Hoisington meets cadre members of the WAC Detachment, Vietnam, October 1967. Left to right: Specialist 4 Rhynell M. Stoabs, Sergeant First Class Betty J. Benson (Acting 1st Sergeant), Colonel Hoisington, Captain Ready, Staff Sergeant Edith L. Efferson, and Private First Class Patricia C. Pewitt. *US Army Photo*

August 21, 2007, at the age of 89. She was buried in a spot of honor at Arlington National Cemetery.

Brigadier General Elizabeth P. Hoisington. *US Army Women's Museum, Fort Lee, Virginia*

★ LEARN MORE ★

An Officer and a Lady: The World War II Letters of Lt. Colonel Betty Bandel, Women's Army Corps edited by Sylvia J. Bugbee (Hanover, NH: University Press of New England, 2004)

Retirement Ceremony for Brigadier General Elizabeth P. Hoisington—film, National Archives and Records Administration. Part I found at https://archive.org/details/gov.archives.arc.34437

Part II found at https://archive.org/details/gov.archives.arc.34438

The Women's Army Corps: 1945–1978 by Bettie J. Morden. Available online at: https://history.army.mil/html/books/030/30-14-1/cmhPub_30-14.pdf

Celia Adolphi

Farm Girl to Major General

Celia stretched her leg as far as it would go to press the clutch and put the "deuce and a half" into gear. The old two-and-a-half-ton army truck rumbled forward. Barely tall enough to see out the windshield, young Celia drove the truck alongside her father as he cut the green feed—corn stalks—which would be used to feed the dairy cows on their Indiana farm. The oldest of three siblings, Celia was no stranger to chores. In addition to driving the truck, Celia helped with the milking and caring for their dairy cows, planting and harvesting soybeans, and canning whatever the family could grow, including tomatoes, corn, green beans, and peas.

Celia also helped with the food preparation. The food on the farm was wholesome and delicious, though there was one thing she did not care for *at all*: creamed tuna on biscuits, a dish she avoids to this day. Mostly, Celia loved her mother's cooking, especially her homemade noodles and chicken. Perhaps that particular meal was what inspired Celia's own fried chicken recipe, which, in 1960, won a championship ribbon at the Indiana State Fair.

Growing up, Celia was busy and proactive. There was a lot of hard work, sure, but a lot of fun times on the farm too. One of Celia's favorite things to do was to read the newspaper to her best friend, a dog named Laddie. With her human family members, Celia enjoyed playing dominoes or a card game called Pit. Celia also loved to play the piano. She had been taking lessons since she was seven years old, just after learning to drive the farm truck. She was sure she would pursue a music career after graduating from Westfield High School. She was wrong. Celia did earn two degrees, but not in music. She also joined the army.

Celia calls herself a late bloomer.

At age 27, she graduated from college with a degree not in music but in dietetics.

She married at age 32.

And, the oldest recruit in her class, she left her husband at home so she could attend the army's basic training course. It was during the summer she turned 34.

Life suddenly sped up. Now Private First Class (PFC) Celia Adolphi,

Celia Adolphi with her dog, Laddie. *Celia Adolphi*

Major General Celia Adolphi. *Celia Adolphi*

she graduated from one of the last all-women enlisted courses. She was now a soldier in the Army Reserve and served as a clerk typist. The "Reserve" status meant that she would continue in her civilian job while contributing to and training for the army. The Vietnam War had just ended, and the army was going through incredible changes. Women had played a limited part in the war, mostly as nurses or in administrative roles. Now, in peacetime, the army sought to integrate the genders much more than they ever had before. The Women's Army Corps (WAC), which had been in existence since World War II, was disestablished on October 20, 1978, a year after Celia completed her basic training course. From then on, men and women would train together, and both would be considered part of the Regular Army.

Within months of enlisting, Celia immediately set to work on her commissioning packet, a process that would allow her to be considered for a position as an officer. Barely a year later, on June 7, 1978, she earned the rank of captain, skipping the usual commission to second lieutenant. The Vietnam War left gaps in the needs of the army, and since Celia already had a master's degree in education and counseling (which she'd earned in 1976), she was promoted to this more elevated rank. About this

TWICE THE CITIZEN!

The idea for a "citizen soldier" is nothing new. On April 23, 1908, the US Congress passed Bill 1424. This established a reserve corps of medical officers who would not be full-time army employees, but who would supply support when needed. Today, the US Army Reserve (USAR) comprises about 20 percent of the total army, or approximately 200,000 men and women from all 50 states and 2 territories. These part-time soldiers hold regular jobs outside the military. In addition, they attend army training one weekend each month—called Battle Assembly—as well as two or more consecutive weeks of training once per year. A member of the USAR can have additional duties or be called to mobilize at any time. When this happens, the soldier goes from part-time status to active duty (full-time status) for the period required.

time she accepted a civilian job at Walter Reed Medical Center and used her degree in dietetics to teach second lieutenants to be dietitians in a hospital setting.

Celia's career took off. Being in one of the last WAC classes may have been the only time Celia was ever a *last* in the army. In the next several years, she launched into a number of army firsts:

)) her first helicopter ride—exhilarating until an unexpected rainstorm picked up and made for a hairy ride

)) a promotion to colonel

》 her first command (for an Army Reserve materiel management center)

》 her first mobilization overseas

Celia made history when her *firsts* expanded to the rest of the army. With her promotion to brigadier general, she was the first female one-star general in the US Quartermaster Corps, a branch of the army that focuses on logistics and support.

Celia did not stop there. She made history a second time when she earned her next promotion. This time, Celia was the first female major general—two stars—in the US Army Reserve.

《《《《《《《《《《《《《《《《《《《《《《《《《 ★ 》》》》》》》》》》》》》》》》》》》》》》》》》

THE QUARTERMASTER CORPS

Like a giant wheel, the spokes of the army provide different functions. There are soldiers whose principal job is to fight in close combat (Infantry), drive and maintain army vehicles (Armored Personnel), or work in communications (the Signal Corps). In addition, the Quartermaster Corps provides supplies and services. Supplies are things like food and equipment. Services range from laundry and shower facilities to burial service for fallen army service members. The Quartermaster Corps provides the logistics for obtaining life support supplies and activities vital to the rest of the army. Approximately 65 percent of the people who serve in the Quartermaster Corps draw from the USAR, meaning that reservists hold down full-time jobs while assisting in these critical areas for the army.

《《《《《《《《《《《《《《《《《《《《《《《《《 ★ 》》》》》》》》》》》》》》》》》》》》》》》》》

Alongside Celia's army career, she spent 32 years working as a civilian for the Department of Defense. After moving from Walter Reed Medical Center to Fort Belvoir, Virginia, and then to the Pentagon, there were some days when Celia had to juggle her civilian and Army Reserve jobs at the same time. In her civilian job, she was responsible for helping develop and change the policy for the entire army food service program.

With a new initiative aimed at developing better physical fitness standards throughout the entire army, Celia helped make significant changes to the foods available to soldiers. For example, she worked to change the "butter law" in the navy, a mandate stating that only butter—not margarine—could be used in service kitchens. (The 1937 law was originally enacted to help sailors get sufficient dairy products in their diet.) In the process of doing this job, Celia discovered that soldiers were being served only whole milk instead of having a low-fat or skim milk option available. Next, she helped lower the sodium content in many of the foods while also helping to mandate that salad bars were to be available at all army facilities. For each of these changes, Celia had to work with policy-makers to change laws so that these healthier alternatives were available.

As if that did not keep her busy enough, Celia's job also required that she make sure there were enough dining facilities everywhere and enough cooks. And that was just her civilian job. As a Reserve Officer, she worked with various units as well. As commander, she participated in all areas of her unit's mission, managing the logistics of supplies and services and other responsibilities.

Amid all of this, when she was still a colonel, Celia got a call. She was being mobilized and would deploy to Hungary and Bosnia with a third of her unit, 70 other men and women. The unit's assignment was to support approximately 8,000 troops already stationed in the area. It was 1996, and the mission was called Operation Joint Endeavor. Celia would command a support unit composed of service members from many nations that was part of a peacekeeping force to provide stability in this volatile region. Celia's unit was part of the second rotation, meaning they were taking over from another unit that would now be going home.

When Celia arrived in Hungary, the first thing she noticed was the cold. Their base of operations was an old Russian SCUD

Women of the 55th Materiel Management Center in support of Operation Joint Endeavor, July 1996–February 1997. First row, left to right: SSG Karen Sheppard, SGT Bernadette Smithen, MSG Mary Champion, CW2 Roxanna Beattie, SFC Diana Royster, SGT Gloria Martin, SFC Nancy Reamy, CPT Shannon Welch, CPT Sharon Roberts, and COL Celia Adolphi (Commander). Second row, left to right: SGT Lana Ray, SPC Kendra Jones, SGT Rhonda Mizell, and SGT Towanda Searles. Third row, left to right: SGT Francis Jackson, SPC Melina Johnson, SPC Cheryl Powers, SFC Nina Walls, SPC Arie Barnes, SPC Terry Campbell, and SFC Julie Counts. *Celia Adolphi Collection, Women's Memorial Foundation Collection*

base. It had been a military installation where Russian soldiers could launch intermediate range missiles called SCUDs. With no central heat or air-conditioning, no indoor toilets or even screens on the windows, it was like living on an old-fashioned farm. "Welcome to our home away from home for the next nine months," Celia told her soldiers. She squared her shoulders. Life here, she realized, was going to be challenging.

Even little things, like showering in the mobile trailer units, took careful planning. With limited facilities, the showers were in almost constant use. Celia often showered at midnight when there was no longer a line to get inside. Afterward, she would fall on her cot in a dead-tired sleep. She had no problem sleeping—the next day would start all too soon.

At zero five hundred (5:00 AM), her alarm would jolt her awake. The day began with a briefing—meeting—with all the senior commanders. Depending on what was going on, the team would dole out the tasks that needed to be accomplished. As a logistics officer, Celia helped ensure that all units had the necessary supplies. Together, she and the others worked out a system of supply using the Hungarian rail line to transport necessary goods to soldiers in the field. The days blended together. When she had a chance to call home, about twice a week, she listened to her husband talk about what was going on in the States and was struck by the enormity of how different life was in this war-torn region. Things she took for granted in the United States, like shopping for groceries or driving on well-maintained roads, were nonexistent here. Like so many others, she did not truly appreciate her home until she was away from it for this extended period.

Months later, when her deployment was over, Celia was on her way to her brigadier general officer promotion. Though busy as a colonel, transitioning to the next rank up, general

LETTERS AND NUMBERS— WHAT DO THEY MEAN?

Staff in the military are identified using a special code. This code, a letter and a number, was first conceived of by Napoleon Bonaparte, emperor of France, and a man who many believe was one of the greatest military leaders of all time. In the 19th century, Napoleon's army used a similar configuration to identify staff. For example, in the army today, anything to do with personnel (transfers, promotions, etc.) is called an S-1 for "staff-1." The same position in the navy is an N-1 and in the air force it is an A-1. The army's S-2 code means a position in intelligence, or gathering and sharing information about enemy activities. An S-3 label deals with the tactical level, or the operation of missions. The coding continues for each of the staff areas and is another way that military personnel identify themselves. For example, an S-4 means logistics support. A J-4 means "joint staff" or that more than one military service area is involved.

officer, took a while to get used to. In fact, after the chief of the Army Reserve called her to let her know she'd been selected for the promotion, it really didn't sink in for a couple of days. She did not realize that things would be radically different. They were. The first thing was that her phone started ringing more than usual. And things only got more hectic when the next promotion happened. When Celia earned her promotion to major general, people started putting news articles on her desk.

FIRST FEMALE RESERVE 2-STAR GENERAL

ARMY RESERVE GETS ITS FIRST WOMAN TWO-STAR GENERAL
ARMY RESERVE HAS RICH HISTORY DESPITE BEING SERVICE
YOUNGSTER
FIRST FEMALE 2-STAR GENERAL

Celia kept her army uniform in her Pentagon office so she could change into it whenever she needed to transition from civilian to army officer. She was now being called to speak at events so often that she put together a binder of all her typed speeches. It was the only way to keep organized when each new invitation came in.

At every function, Celia highlighted one important message—the role of women in the army. "They [military women] have really been out there on the cutting edge, willing to take risks when it wasn't popular to take risks, or be commanders, or to step up the plate and do things," she told one interviewer.

Celia received so many awards and accolades for her service it was hard to keep track of them. For example, she earned "Hall of Fame" status on three separate occasions: from the US Army Quartermaster Corps, from the Defense Logistics Agency, and from her old high school in Indiana.

Finally, Celia retired from the Army Reserve on June 12, 2003. However, she did not give up her service to the public. Today, Celia still receives frequent invitations to speak at various events. She also serves on various boards. When recently asked what she misses most about the army, Celia did not hesitate. "The camaraderie with mission-oriented officers and NCOs [noncommissioned officers]; opportunities to help others excel in their careers."

Indeed, what caused that plucky little farm girl to excel in her own career? Was it driving the old army truck on the farm? Was it having the courage to persevere—and succeed—in a mostly male army? Was it sticking with a task and getting the job done *no matter what?* Celia Adolphi, farm girl to major general, does one thing right: she does not let anything stop her.

★ LEARN MORE ★

"Former WACs Remember Women's Army," www.army.mil
    /article/14098/former-wacs-remember-womens-army
United States Army Reserve, www.army.mil/reserve
United States Army Women's Museum, www.awm.lee.army.mil

LeAnn Swieczkowski

Petite and Powerful

"Come on Ski! Come on Ski!"

LeAnn was vaguely aware of people yelling in the background, but her focus was on pumping her arms down, up, down, up. She had one goal: to complete as many push-ups as physically possible in two minutes.

"One minute," the drill sergeant called. LeAnn had knocked out 66 push-ups. She kept going. 80, 85, 90 . . . 100.

"Time!"

LeAnn rolled over and sat up. She'd done it; she'd broken her own personal record of 93 push-ups in two minutes! Not only that, LeAnn had maxed the standard for *anyone*, male or female, her age or younger.

When LeAnn Swieczkowski (Swi-COW-ski) joined the army, she was in superb physical shape. She continued to hone this ability. While serving on the staff at Fort Leavenworth in 1987, she broke three records at the World Powerlifting Federation competition. Weighing just 97 pounds herself, she was able to squat 175 pounds, bench-press 115 pounds, and deadlift 265 pounds.

The *Pentagram*, a newspaper internal to the Pentagon, featured a story on this amazing powerhouse: "Since entering the military in June of 1981 at age 31, Swieczkowski has maxed every physical fitness test she has taken." With an exterior that could be deceiving—the petite, soft-spoken woman was just 5 foot 2 inches tall—LeAnn possessed a rare strength and determination. The Army's Physical Fitness Test—the APFT—was just one measure.

LeAnn always knew that being a soldier was her dream job. It was just surprising that it took her so long to join the ranks. All her uncles and one aunt had military backgrounds. The

BE ALL YOU CAN BE

Two minutes of push-ups. Two minutes of sit-ups. A two-mile run.

Twice a year, the army requires every soldier in the force to pass a fitness test. Each event has a maximum score of 100 points. The current standard for the full 100 points in push-ups for females between ages 17 and 21 is 42 push-ups in two minutes. The minimum requirement (which earns 60 points), is 19 push-ups. For this same age category, women will max the standard if they run two miles in under 15 minutes and 36 seconds. For females and males, the sit-ups requirement is the same: 82 sit-ups in two minutes will earn a perfect score of 100 points.

men served in World War II, Korea, and Vietnam. LeAnn's aunt had been a WAC (Women's Army Corps). Even LeAnn's only brother served in Germany—at the same time that rock star Elvis Presley was enlisted. As far back as she could remember, LeAnn wanted to follow in these family members' footsteps.

In 1967 LeAnn graduated from Madison High School in Madison Heights, Michigan. She had applied for—but not received—a military scholarship. *Okay, Plan B*, she thought. She immersed herself in studying for a bachelor's of psychology, paying the whole way herself. (Typical for LeAnn, she kept going and later earned two more degrees: a master's in counseling and a master's in management.) Her dream to enter the army simmered quietly in the background, but life got busy, and LeAnn kept postponing the decision to enlist.

It seemed like before she knew it, LeAnn was 31 years old. She sat down and thought hard about her lifelong passion to be a soldier. She knew she wanted to go to Officer Candidate School (OCS) and that she would be crushed if she did not accomplish this life goal. The problem was that she was now past the age limit. Her only option was to apply for a special waiver and hope to be accepted. *It's do or die*, she told herself. LeAnn filled out the necessary paperwork and thankfully received the appropriate age waiver. She enlisted in the army on November 10, 1981.

There were things LeAnn liked about basic training and others she disliked. She enjoyed the drills and physical training, and she also valued the camaraderie she found with the other college "gals." There were five older women who, like LeAnn, had completed at least one degree and would head to Officer Candidate School after basic. LeAnn could not say she enjoyed when the drill sergeants yelled and hollered, but she found that being older and more mature helped. She was less intimidated by all the shouting than some of the younger recruits.

On the other hand, the course had its challenges. For one thing, the heat during July and August at Fort Jackson, South Carolina, was at first unbearable. For another, there was a lack of privacy in nearly everything—something LeAnn was not used to at all. First was the shower situation. Since there was only one showerhead and a limited time for cleaning up, personal showers became a shared activity with several women moving in a circle, lathering up when it wasn't their turn under the water. It was unpleasant—funny, but unpleasant. Then there were the sleeping arrangements. LeAnn had a bottom bunk, and at any time during the short night (usually six or seven hours), there could be interruptions such as the annoyance of another woman's snoring or a fire drill or simulated attack. LeAnn learned to pop instantly awake.

Basic training was often uncomfortable, but LeAnn understood the rationale for the manufactured stress. There was a purpose for everything, and tension was part of making tough soldiers. After all, this training was preparing the men and women for real combat. *We protect our country,* LeAnn thought to herself. *We can't have anyone who isn't prepared.*

The mornings started with physical training—no problem for LeAnn since she was in such great shape—followed by cleaning up and chores. After a march of one to five miles, her company arrived in the training field. They might eat breakfast there or be given a strict two minutes to bolt down some food in the mess hall before they left. Field exercises included maneuvering through obstacle courses such as the barbed wire course or practicing weapons training.

"Hey, Ski! Come over here and show us how to do this." Early on, LeAnn became the person instructors used to demonstrate new tasks. Today "this" referred to Australian rappelling. LeAnn was going to show the others how to rappel down

Rifle practice with M-16, Fort Jackson, South Carolina. *LeAnn Swieczkowski*

Confidence course. *LeAnn Swieczkowski*

a wall—*headfirst!* Inside LeAnn was shaking, but soldiers could not show any weakness. There was no way she would give anyone an excuse to drum her out. She took a breath. Jumped.

Next there was another challenge; LeAnn would participate in biological and chemical training.

"When you go inside there's going to be real tear gas," the drill sergeant told them. "Now practice. You have nine seconds to put on your mask."

LeAnn pulled her mask from the canvas pouch strapped to her waist. She fitted the mask over her head and cleared it, testing to make sure the seal was good. They practiced again and again until everyone could do the task in under nine seconds.

The platoon stood in formation outside the gas chamber. They were five soldiers across and six deep. "Right Face!" LeAnn followed the marching orders until the formation became a line. She told herself not to be nervous. *It has to be OK*, LeAnn told herself. *They can't have us do anything too terrible, right?*

"Remember, once your mask is off, don't touch your eyes. Now, GO!"

LeAnn and the others filed inside. The drill sergeant closed the door behind them and placed a couple of pill-sized tablets in a metal pie tin over a flame. Poisonous CS gas filled the room, and the drill sergeant gave the signal. LeAnn took off her mask. Immediately her eyes stung and her nose and throat felt like they were burning. Her exposed skin stung, too, and her nose and eyes began to stream liquid.

"What's your name, soldier?" the drill sergeant barked.

"What's your social security number?"

"Tell me the ranks of all sergeants."

LeAnn choked out her answers, resisting the urge to rub her eyes. Every second was a torment. Finally, the time was up. LeAnn rushed from the room. Outside she gulped fresh air and

Gas chamber, waiting to go in. *LeAnn Swieczkowski*

staggered away from the building, flapping her arms to remove the toxin from her clothing. Soon the burning dissipated. Strangely, she felt ecstatic. She had done it! She had qualified in the tear gas exercise!

Passing the army's basic training course was LeAnn's first hurdle. Next was Officer Candidate School, followed by other courses including Airborne School—a course designed to teach soldiers how to parachute from airplanes. The army assigned her a specialization—LeAnn was to be a military police officer (MP). When she received her orders, she learned that she would be working at Fort Leavenworth, Kansas, the United States Disciplinary Barracks.

The staff at the USDB was mostly MPs, but the inmates were from all ranks and branches of the military, though all men. One of LeAnn's jobs there was to document inmate crimes in preparation for a custody board to determine further punishment.

(((((((((((((((((((((((((((((((((((((★)))))))))))))))))))))))))))))))))))))

CHEMICAL WARFARE

On April 22, 1915, outside Ypres, Belgium, a yellow-green cloud of toxic gas drifted toward Allied soldiers stationed in trenches. It was not tear gas but chlorine, the same substance that is used in swimming pools and in our drinking water to make it safe. However, in large quantities and thick concentrations as it was used in World War I, chlorine gas is deadly. Heavier than regular air, the gas clung to the ground near Ypres and spread across the battlefield and into the trenches. Soldiers began choking, screaming, and dying in large numbers. Today most countries have signed agreements making the use of chlorine gas and other chemical weapons in battle illegal. However, US soldiers train to deal with a chemical attack—just in case.

(((((((((((((((((((((((((((((((((((((★)))))))))))))))))))))))))))))))))))))

Some of the crimes included fighting, smuggling drugs, or threatening the commandant in writing. If found guilty, offenders could have time added to their sentence or they could have privileges taken away, even clothing and blankets. They might be condemned to bread and water for a couple of days, or for serious offenses, there was solitary confinement. As part of her training, LeAnn had to learn how to subdue an unruly prisoner. This was done in a five-person team—one person for each arm and leg as well as the inmate's head.

What the heck am I doing here? LeAnn whispered to herself when she first arrived. Her office was in the basement of the old prison complex. Every day she went through several security measures to get to work. She walked through the first gate. In

⟪⟪⟪⟪⟪⟪⟪⟪⟪⟪⟪⟪ ★ ⟫⟫⟫⟫⟫⟫⟫⟫⟫⟫⟫⟫

OUR MISSION—YOUR FUTURE

Congress established the United States Disciplinary Barracks (USDB) in 1874. Construction began the next year, mostly by prison workers. The facility, made from stone and brick, was nicknamed "The Castle." It could hold up to 1,500 inmates, each convicted by court martial. A new, modern facility opened in 2002 with a capacity for 515 offenders. The maximum-security prison houses enlisted offenders who are serving sentences over 10 years as well as convicted commissioned officers and those whose crimes threaten national security.

Inside the prison, there is no internet allowed, but inmates can watch some TV and there is a library and fitness facilities. Some offenders have jobs that can pay a small amount per hour. The mission of the facility is to prepare the inmates for life back in the civilian world. This prison serves men only. Women are incarcerated at the Naval Consolidated Brig in Miramar, California. That does not stop women from working at the USDB, however. In 2002 Colonel Colleen McGuire was the first female commandant of this prison.

⟪⟪⟪⟪⟪⟪⟪⟪⟪⟪⟪⟪ ★ ⟫⟫⟫⟫⟫⟫⟫⟫⟫⟫⟫⟫

this holding area, this first gate had to close before the second gate could open. There were three access points like this. She was also subject to a metal detector and physical searches. Security was tight, and it was a good thing—the facility included some of the military's worst offenders. It was shocking, then, when LeAnn learned that two medium-security prisoners had escaped.

LeAnn received a call. Everyone was ordered back to work immediately. LeAnn helped search the barracks, but when it was clear that the men were not hiding inside, the search expanded to outside the prison walls. As events unfolded, it was LeAnn's job to investigate the escape and document exactly what happened.

LeAnn's second military career was as an army public affairs specialist. She worked for the next nine years in that role, including overseas duty. In 1992 her skills with writing and leadership were needed for a crisis halfway across the world. LeAnn mobilized to Somalia.

Hampered by looters and the violence of clashing Somali clans, troops were called in to help with food distribution efforts.

OVER THE WALL

Inside the military prison there were five cadre counts every day. If the total number of prisoners did not add up, the duty officer initiated a recount. On Friday, January 9, 1987, all were present for the 4:30 PM head count. However, at the 12:30 AM count, the total came up two prisoners short. Kenneth E. Davis and John Yarbrough had waited in a blind spot in the yard until the guards changed shifts. They climbed up a drainpipe and scaled a 20-foot wall. From there they climbed three more fences, each topped with barbed wire. Over 100 officials conducted a manhunt to apprehend the escapees. Finally, with the help of a helicopter's spotlight, the men were caught fleeing by foot along a railroad track. They were returned to the prison, where they awaited further disciplinary action.

Attached to the First Marine Expeditionary Force, LeAnn arrived in Somalia on December 13. Her job was to serve as a US forces spokesperson, overseeing communications between the media and US troops. Even by army standards, life there was harsh—and dangerous. For LeAnn, it was a matter of doing her best under difficult circumstances.

In the capital of Somalia, Mogadishu, the former American University was a large, round building now devastated by the conflict. The room LeAnn moved into had three walls and no roof. The last occupants had been goats, so the first thing LeAnn did was to help clean it out. Cots replaced hay, and she and seven other women moved in. Somalia was like nothing she had ever seen. LeAnn compared life there to life inside the Fort Leavenworth Disciplinary Barracks. Unlike the barracks, there were no flushing toilets, no running water or showers, no telephone service or TV, and almost no privacy. There was also constant noise.

Instead of taking a shower, LeAnn dumped a canteen of water over her head. She poured more water over herself to rinse off the soap. Since she had neglected to bring flip-flops, she stood in the mud until she scavenged a wooden pallet to stand on. She hunted for other things to use as well. Plastic milk crates became a dresser, and she found a bucket for handwashing her clothes. LeAnn wrote in a letter home, "Another major benefit, (if there are any in prison), to being within the confines of the disciplinary barracks; as opposed to being stationed in Mogadishu, Somalia, is that inmates don't have to fear ambushes, sniper fire, rocket propelled grenades, or mortar rounds."

Just outside the university base stood a two-story building. It housed approximately 300 Somali family members. It was also a perfect vantage point for Somali snipers. As a matter of everyone's safety, the army decided to relocate the families and demolish the building. Expecting the press to show up, LeAnn put on her Kevlar helmet and bulletproof vest. She packed her 9mm gun—loaded—and a camcorder to document the events. She headed to the building.

LeAnn was at the scene when a Somali man came up to her and shook his cane at her, spewing a spate of angry words that she could not understand. She turned back to her filming, but not before noticing that the man held a machete in his other hand. Indeed, violence threatened the efforts of the many

CRISIS IN SOMALIA

On August 15, 1992, the United Nations announced a humanitarian relief mission in Somalia. The country was in turmoil amid civil war and a terrible drought. Hundreds of thousands of Somalis were on the brink of starvation. The Somali government was nonexistent, and the United Nations called for relief from countries all over the world. However, food distribution efforts were not easy. Looters and organized militants stole most of the donated food and often exchanged it for weapons. Critical supplies were not going to the people who needed them most. The United States deployed combat troops to secure the delivery of food. However, despite the presence of peacekeeping soldiers, violence continued. For example, on October 3–4, 1993, 18 US soldiers died in the capital city of Mogadishu during an assault to find the leader of one of the rebel forces. Today, poverty continues to plague this country located on the eastern coast of Africa.

nations stationed in Somalia to distribute supplies. More than once, LeAnn was in the field of fire. When militants killed 24 Pakistani soldiers in an ambush on June 5, 1993, soldiers like LeAnn were no longer allowed to leave the installation.

LeAnn's time in Somalia was only seven months, but it changed her. Back in the States, she was out running one day when a construction crew started their equipment nearby. LeAnn dove into the bushes. She had to train herself to react appropriately to loud noises. There were other effects of her experience too. She started to conserve water by turning off the shower between lathering up and washing off. Rather than throw things out, she reconditioned tools and equipment around the house—something she still does to this day.

Stateside, LeAnn continued to work in public affairs until, after 20 years, she retired as a major in 2001. Her time in the service reinforced her belief in herself and strengthened her capacity for leadership. Today she volunteers with several committees in and around her community in Charlotte, North Carolina. When she looks back on the things she did in the army, LeAnn

Major Swieczkowski at the Pentagon.
LeAnn Swieczkowski

shakes her head. *Was that really me?* she asks herself. Then she recalls, "But folks tell me I'm strong and so I appear to be."

★ LEARN MORE ★

National Museum of the United States Army, https://army history.org/about-the-museum
Women's Army Corps Veteran's Association, www.army women.org/wacHistory.shtml

PART IV

Current Conflicts

War in Modern Times

★ ★ ★ ★ ★

By the turn of the 21st century, the US Army had integrated women into all but a fraction of the occupational specialties and career fields available in the military. After the terrorist attacks in New York, Washington, and Pennsylvania on September 11, 2001, over 300,000 women were deployed to Afghanistan and Iraq. As of February 2019, over 1,000 of these women had been wounded. And 170 were killed. Still others became prisoners of war.

Clearly, women were serving on dangerous missions. With an undefined battle front, anyone could come under attack and there was no longer a behind-the-lines position of relative safety. Yet during the conflict in the Middle East, an outdated ruling from the Department of Defense was still in place, causing a disconnect between policy and the reality of women's roles in actual military operations. This was the 1994 Direct Ground Combat Definition and Assignment Rule. The regulation stated in part, "Service members are eligible to be assigned to all positions for which they are qualified, except that women shall be excluded from assignment to units below the brigade level whose primary mission is to engage in direct combat on the ground."

If this ruling were implemented as specified, women would not be serving in hostile territory where the likelihood of an ambush or roadside bombing was a daily threat. The fact was that they were. Leigh Ann Hester's team, Raven 42, was not the only military police unit that included women. It was not the only unit responsible for ensuring the safe transport of supply convoys through volatile enemy lands. However, Raven 42 was a stark example of how women were engaged in direct combat, despite the ruling against it. In March 2005 Leigh Ann participated in a firefight that left members of her team gravely wounded and 27 Anti-Iraqi Forces (AIF) dead. In an interview with CBS shortly after the incident, Leigh Ann stated, "You don't really have time to feel anything. It's not a man or woman thing. You have to act like a soldier and respond like a soldier and that's what we did."

War in the Middle East underscored the value of women in the military. As thousands of women answered the call to defend their country, people like Brigadier General Deborah Kotulich and Captain Stephanie Lincoln helped to change the policy of barring women from certain military professions. Just two examples of exceptional leaders, these female soldiers commanded both women and men and proved that once again, qualified women made gender a nonissue. When Chief Warrant Officer 5 Mary Hostetler became the first female criminal investigations agent in a war zone, it was obvious that the law needed to change. It did. In January 2013 the Department of Defense eliminated the 1994 Direct Ground Combat Definition and Assignment Rule. They determined that full implementation would take place in three years—unless military leaders could develop a case for any exceptions.

Each branch carefully studied the effects of including women in all aspects of military assignments. The army conducted the US Army Gender Integration Study and concluded that full integration would enhance, not weaken, this military branch. Finally, on January 1, 2016, the Pentagon removed the last obstacle for qualified women. Weeks earlier, Ash Carter, secretary of defense, had signed a bill directing that all military branches open positions to women who met the uncompromised standard—no exceptions. In a statement reported by the *New York Times*, he explained, "In the 21st century that requires drawing strength from the broadest possible pool of talent. This includes women."

Mary Hostetler

Citizen Soldier—Rock Steady

"There is nothing more awe inspiring than public servants who are willing to place themselves in harm's way for the protection of others."

Jimmy Panetta, newly elected member of the US House of Representatives, stood as he addressed the members of Congress on February 14, 2017. He was honoring Mary Hostetler on her retirement from the US Army. Both he and Mary were from California, but there was another reason Jimmy chose to include this statement in the day's Congressional Record. Mary had been one of the team officers in charge of security for Jimmy's father, Leon, during the last year Leon had been the secretary of defense.

A few weeks earlier, Mary had been in Jimmy's office at the US Capitol building. The two of them had exchanged mutual congratulations—to Jimmy for his position as representative for the state of California, and to Mary for her retirement from the US Army. She had been in Washington, DC, on January 7, 2017,

DO WHAT HAS TO BE DONE

Living this motto, today the Criminal Investigations Command operates out of Quantico, Virginia. The primary mission of this organization is to provide the army with expert special agents who investigate crimes within the army. For this reason, the agents wear civilian clothes outside the office and they do not refer to their rank. This could jeopardize a case where they were investigating a person of higher rank.

The command also trains agent teams to provide protective services for various key leaders. With roots dating before the Civil War, the organization started when the army hired private companies like the Pinkerton Detective Agency to investigate criminal acts within its ranks. Shortly after the army established the Military Police Corps during World War I, General John Pershing directed that a Criminal Investigations Division (CID) be created. Today's CID comes from a restructuring of the Corps on September 17, 1971. About 2,000 soldiers and citizens now work for the CID around the world, along with approximately 900 special agents. When these agents work on protective detail, there are different teams assigned to different tasks. One team might be the advance team—they work with local authorities ahead of time to set up safe routes and venues. Another team may provide security at the "principal's" home—the person receiving the protection. A third team travels with this leader wherever he or she goes.

to celebrate that fact at a ceremony at the Women in Military Service for America Memorial.

On the airplane back to her home in California, Mary thought over her incredible career. For the past four decades, she had served in the army as a military police officer (MP), a criminal investigator, special agent (CID), and as a supervisory criminal investigator, special agent. She had risen to the rare and prestigious rank of chief warrant officer 5 (CW5), a position designed for technical and tactical experts.

Mary knew the army had given her unique opportunities she never would have gotten in the civilian world—along with an unequivocal pride for her service to the United States. She had ridden camels in Egypt, lived in a presidential palace in Iraq, and traveled all over the world, including to places like Israel, Singapore, and Chile. Throughout her career, she had interacted with top leaders and held positions of enormous responsibility. Yet, despite all her accomplishments, Mary never lost sight of the

simple reason she enlisted in the first place: she wanted to stand up to the United States' enemies. And she knew she could do it.

Chief Warrant Officer 5 Mary Hostetler, command chief for the 200th Military Police Command, Fort Meade, Maryland, October 16, 2016. *US Army Reserve photo by Master Sgt. Michel Sauret*

Mary nodded to herself. There was something else she knew for certain: "The best thing I have ever done is wear the army uniform."

Mary reflected on another thing: her life had not always been easy. She had experienced tough challenges and real danger, but she had made it through each of these difficult times with perseverance and faith. At every roadblock, Mary had told herself to find a way past it, to look for the next opportunity and not let the current circumstances stop her. Oh, yes, Mary had come a long way from the skinny girl who grew up on a humble farm near Wooster, Ohio.

Mary was born on October 16, 1956, at 6:56 PM. Her mother teased Mary that she did not want to come into this world since she was born three weeks past her due date. As Mary grew into an adventurous young girl, Mary's mother said they were poor, but Mary did not see it. Money was tight, but to Mary, the farm where she was raised was idyllic and her family, next to perfect. They were six miles south of Wooster, Ohio, on a 15-acre farm with several Amish relatives nearby. (Mary's father was Amish, and her mother was Irish.)

Mary loved life on the farm. She enjoyed the freedom of being outside, and she liked doing her chores and being around animals. Not many others she knew had their own pony. Mary did. There were also dogs, cats, cows, sheep, chickens, rabbits, and even turkeys on the farm. Mary approached her chores like fun games. Since she was the youngest and littlest, Mary got to drive the tractor during haying season. When she milked the cow, Mary made a game of avoiding Bossy's swishing tail— though if she missed, the cow's tail could wrap painfully around her head.

Mary had four siblings—a sister 15 years older who was like a second mom; a brother who was three years older; and twins just one year ahead of her. One of the twins had a profound mental disability, and Mary, even though she was the youngest, often helped care for him. Bobby was her first lesson in defending the underdog, and she became his fierce protector. When she first attended school, she felt terribly guilty for abandoning him.

Going to school was indeed an adjustment. Mary eventually got used to it when she discovered new friends and a new passion—softball. There were no girls' teams available, however, so Mary organized games with the boys. She and another girl played at recess and after school, except when there were formal Little League games. For those, Mary was relegated to bat girl. It was against the rules for girls to play.

One day in fifth grade there was a fight. When the class bully decided to pick on a boy named Eli for being Amish, Mary decided not to let him. When the fight was over, Mary sat in the principal's office with rumpled clothes and mud-caked hair. Her mother had been called in and was sitting beside her. The whole time the principal, Mr. Dunham, admonished Mary, he shook his head, but not because he felt it was wrong to defend Eli. "We've *never* had such unladylike behavior!" he exclaimed. Fighting, apparently, was for boys only.

Mary was embarrassed to go back to class in her disheveled state, but she was not sorry for her actions. This was who she was—she was not afraid to fight for what was right. That day Mary fought her first bully and perhaps laid down the groundwork for a career in protecting others from being victims, including herself.

As Mary grew up, she began to admire the job of a police officer. During sixth grade, a police detective named Paul Garver came to her classroom to talk about safety. Mary was intrigued and impressed. What would it be like to wear a police uniform?

She thought, too, about the Vietnam War and wondered about being a soldier. Her mother had been writing letters to three cousins fighting overseas. When she was 17 years old, Mary decided to enlist as a marine, but she was underage and needed her parents' permission. They refused. According to family legend, Mary's mother may or may not have met the recruiter at their door with a shotgun.

Mary put the military on hold until she could join without her parents' consent. When she finally attended her swearing-in ceremony for the Army Reserve, it was July 22, 1976. She was the first woman ever to enlist with the 447th Military Police Company out of Wooster.

Two months later, Mary took her first plane ride. She was on her way to the basic training course at Fort Jackson. Her class, she found out later, was part of an army experiment called the Basic Initial Entry Training Test (BIET). Normally, women had their own training facility and a separate program developed exclusively for the Women's Army Corps. For the BIET study, the army had selected two companies of female recruits to train on the same schedule as a battalion of men. Could these women succeed at standards identical to the requirements for men?

Mary, along with one other woman, proved that they could. She passed—and exceeded—the same benchmarks as the men in her class. (Today, there are different standards for men and women.) Next Mary attended specialized training to become a military police officer. She graduated at 20 years old.

Mary was now part of the Army Reserve. She would serve one weekend every month and during a two-week training camp over the summer in order to maintain force readiness and support the Regular Army. Of course, active duty orders could come at any time. If this happened, she would take leave from

Private First Class Mary Hostetler, 447th Military Police Company, in an M151A1 army jeep at the Lima Army Tank Plant in Lima, Ohio, 1977. *Mary Hostetler*

her civilian job to complete the mission full time. That was fine—serving her country was what Mary signed up for.

In her civilian life, Mary attended community college. She also explored the idea of being an Ohio State Highway Patrol officer once she turned 21 and met the age requirement. She put in her application and passed every test except one. Mary was five feet, seven and three-quarters inches tall. To be in the Ohio State Highway Patrol, you had to be at least five feet, eight inches tall. The army had had no such requirement! Mary needed to refocus. What would she do now? She applied—and was accepted—to work as a state police officer at the Ohio Apple Creek Developmental Center, a facility for the mentally challenged. She followed this with a job as a welfare fraud investigator.

Mary's first mobilization came in 1980. Still part of the 447th Company, she traveled to Fort McCoy in Wisconsin. The army had set up a Cuban refugee resettlement center there to accommodate an influx of men, women, and children fleeing Cuba and the country's harsh dictator, Fidel Castro. Mary, a sergeant now, put on her army uniform for military police duty from 7:00 PM to 7:00 AM. This included patrolling the grounds, stationary

POLICING, IN THE MILITARY AND OUT

With the establishment of the Women's Army Auxiliary Corps (WAAC) during World War II, women trained as military police (MPs) mainly to supervise other female soldiers. The army did not officially accept women into the Military Police Corps until 1975, while still excluding them from combat positions. In 1988 Linda Bray, 29 years old, was the commander of the 988th Military Police Company. When her unit deployed to Panama a year later, she found herself and her unit in an unexpected firefight. Captain Bray became the first woman to lead men into combat, spurring the debate about allowing women to serve in combat positions. Though this experience proved that women were *already* serving in combat, it took a long time for that fact to be formally accepted.

And it wasn't just the army. The Ohio State Highway Patrol was also slow to accept women into its ranks. It was not until 1976 that this organization allowed women to enter the force. Two women entered the 100th Cadet Class after the force replaced the word *patrolman* with *trooper*. One of the women, Dianne Harris, earned her commission. On February 4, 1977, she became the first female trooper in Ohio.

guard duty, and supervisory duties. With few women in the army at the time, Mary was one of four women serving for the 447th, and the only woman assigned to night duty.

When the mission ended, Mary volunteered for another active duty position and was soon stationed in Hawai'i as an army recruiter. She served a three-year term until, honorably discharged, her life took another major turn. This time, Mary was back in Ohio when she ran into the officer who had initially sworn her in when she first enlisted into the 447th. Greg Long had remained a friend over the years, and now as the commander of the Army Reserve Criminal Investigations Company (CID) in Columbus, Ohio, he asked Mary if she wanted a job.

"Would I!" Mary exclaimed. *Being a special agent, a criminal investigator for the CID is the cream of the crop! They are the detectives*

FREEDOM FLOTILLA

On April 20, 1980, Cuba's dictator, Fidel Castro, announced that anyone wishing to leave the country could do so. Conditions in Cuba were poor, so thousands crowded to Cuba's Muriel Harbor to meet US relatives and friends in rented boats. Nearly 125,000 refugees sailed the 90 miles to Florida in what some called a "Freedom Flotilla." The United States took them in, but scrambled to set up resettlement camps around the country. On May 29 Fort McCoy accepted the first group of Cuban men, women, and children. The people who came often had nothing but the clothes they were wearing. There were also a number of criminals in the crowd. Fidel Castro had emptied prisons when he allowed people to leave the country.

of the army military police, she said to herself. She filled out the necessary paperwork and applied for a top-security clearance. In late 1986 the CID accepted Mary for training.

Mary's specialty was protective services. She attended more training, including a driving course to learn what to do in case of a threat. She learned to do bootlegs (a maneuver to reverse the direction of a vehicle in minimal time) and J-turns (a 180-degree turn while a vehicle is traveling backward). Because of her skill and dedication in all areas of the training, her superiors gave Mary more and more responsibility. Shortly after graduation, she was assigned protective detail for Secretary of Defense (SECDEF) Dick Cheney. She headed to Fort Belvoir, Virginia.

The job was exciting, but stressful too. Mary wore civilian clothes when she went with the SECDEF to Congress, to the White House, to the Pentagon, and to various events and formal dinners. She was *right there*—in the know of whatever was going on. Her job was to prepare for the worst and to be on the constant lookout for potential threats. When Secretary Cheney had to be somewhere, she had to get him there *exactly* on time—if it was 3:30, it could not be 3:29 or 3:31. Mary's day started three or four hours before meeting the SECDEF for his round of activities and ended approximately that long after he had finished. It was challenging, but she tried to embrace these challenges. She told herself, *Challenges can defeat you, or they can create strength.*

Mary grew stronger.

In 1992 Mary went to Warrant Officer Candidate School and graduated with recognition for being the most physically fit. Over the next several years, she rose to the very highest warrant officer rank, one of only 116 in the entire Army Reserve. She continued to work on select missions, providing protective detail for other top leaders and doing criminal investigations work.

At 46 years old, Mary received new orders. She was mobilizing to the Middle East with the 375th CID Detachment out of Columbus, Ohio. As she prepared to leave, Mary thought she would be investigating war crimes while over in Iraq. The mission changed. She became a member of the team in charge of protecting the top leaders, including the US presidential envoy to Iraq, Paul Bremer. Mary was a trailblazer once again—she was the first female CID agent to serve in this role in a combat zone.

Iraq looked like a disaster zone. On her trip by convoy to the city of Baghdad, Mary passed through small villages with homes built from mud and brick and people so poor that they did not have shoes. Despite this, the people were mostly friendly and gave the American soldiers a thumbs-up. There were exceptions. More than once people would draw their fingers across their throats as they stared at Mary and the others. It was a country in turmoil, and Mary's job was to help stabilize it.

In the city of Baghdad, Mary moved into the old Republican Palace, part of Saddam Hussein's former stronghold. The recent bombings had blown out the windows, and looters had carried off most of the valuables. Initially there was no electricity or air-conditioning and everyone's cot included a mosquito net. On the second floor where Mary slept, the heat could be unbearable—a good 15 degrees warmer than even the scorching temperature outside. When the plumbing was not working—about half the time—it took Mary 17 minutes to walk one way to a bathroom outside. Until shower trailers were delivered, Mary had to make do the best she could. Even when the trailers did arrive, they were coed with only certain hours for females. She often seemed to be out on a mission during those times.

Basic necessities were indeed a challenge. Every morning Mary filled up on protein such as hard-boiled eggs. She could be out for a 12-hour stretch with almost no opportunity to eat or use the bathroom. However, with temperatures well over 100 degrees, most of the hot water she drank was processed as sweat.

Then there was the stress of the job itself. Since there was no government to regulate weapons sales, any Iraqi citizen could purchase a gun. Between the heat and the equipment she carried, Mary felt like a cement truck, though she again wore civilian clothes as part of the protective detail. She had an MP4 rifle with her at all times, and she also packed a 9mm pistol. She carried at least 144 rounds of ammunition. The mood in the country was tense with an ever-present potential for violence. Mary

THE GREEN ZONE

People commonly refer to Iraq's International Zone in Baghdad as the Green Zone. It is a nearly four-square-mile area where the United States and its allies set up a provisional government when they first invaded the country. Before arriving, this area was the center of the Iraqi government under dictator Saddam Hussein. It is where the Republican Palace is located, the building where coalition forces initially set up their headquarters. The Green Zone is heavily fortified. There are high T-walls—steel reinforced concrete walls made to withstand most attacks—and barbed wire fences surrounding the district. Entry checkpoints include guards, and many areas are restricted to the public. Considered the safest place in Baghdad during the conflict, the area was nicknamed "the bubble."

had to stay alert at all times, making sure that any local tension did not turn dangerous.

Mary's mission in Iraq was not easy, but it was vital. Somehow, the coalition had to help the Iraqi people reconstruct their country. Somehow, Mary's team had to prevent other terrible things from happening. When the tour was over, the army deemed her deployment a success. She earned a Bronze Star Medal for completing over 600 daily missions.

Changed, and more appreciative than ever that she was American, Mary went back to her civilian job in the States. She continued to serve as a reservist when called up for various important missions. For example, Mary helped provide security to Secretary of Defense Leon Panetta during his last year in office. It was a hectic time. Mary worked 24 hours a day, with maybe one day off per week. She also served during another mobilization to Afghanistan.

Finally, one day it was all over. After 40 years, Mary retired from the army.

November 1, 2016, was a day filled with a deep sense of pride and accomplishment. With her retirement papers in hand, Mary reflected on her incredible army career. Had there been challenges? Absolutely. Had she sometimes felt inadequate to the task? Of course. However, she had always talked herself through these difficulties. "There will be challenges in your life," she said. "When things don't go your way, focus on the opportunities available to you and you will carve a path with more rewards than you can imagine." Mary was grateful, more than ever, that she had stayed on the army path.

Today, Mary continues to work for the Presidio Police Department in California, but anticipates that she will retire from this civilian job soon. She carries a challenge coin, a personal token that commemorates her time in the military. On the

Chief Warrant Officer 5 Mary Hostetler gives her remarks during her retirement ceremony held at the Women in Military Service for America Memorial on January 7, 2017, in Arlington, Virginia. *US Army Reserve photo by Sgt. 1st Class Sun Vega*

coin is the CID motto: Do what has to be done. Indeed, throughout her life Mary has done what is necessary, no matter what. Rock steady—this is who Mary Hostetler worked to become.

☆ LEARN MORE ☆

My Year in Iraq: The Struggle to Build a Future of Hope by Ambassador L. Paul Bremer III (New York, NY: Simon & Schuster, 2006)

US Army Criminal Investigation Command, www.cid.army.mil /mission.html

Stephanie Lincoln

Pretty Good at This Army Thing

Stephanie Lincoln held an M16A1 rifle in front of her. She finally had a chance to fire it, after carrying it around—even sleeping with it—for the previous several days. At first, the gun had terrified her. *Safety, safety, safety,* she told herself now and mentally went over the four fundamentals of marksmanship: steady position, aiming, breath control, and trigger squeeze. She double-checked that the weapon was on "safe" before she inserted a loaded cartridge magazine and chambered a round. She faced the target and placed the gun against her shoulder. It felt cold and heavy, though according to the manual, the weapon, including the magazine, was less than 10 pounds. She switched to "semi" and took aim, aligning the target along the sight of the gun. She controlled her breath like she had practiced—and pulled the trigger.

Not bad! Stephanie kept her face blank, but inside she was ecstatic. If only her dad could see her now! Something shifted in her brain. She thought, *I'm pretty good at this army thing.* For the first time during basic combat training, she was 100 percent glad that her life had taken this path. It sure was not what she thought she'd be doing when she was a senior in high school— no, this was much, much better.

\(\!\!\(\!\(\!\(\!\(\!\(\!\(\!\(\!\(\!\(\!\(\!\(\!\(\!\(\!\(\! ★ \)

BASIC COMBAT—
MENTAL AND PHYSICAL TRAINING

After an introductory period, the basic training course includes three phases: Red, White, and Blue. During the first phase recruits learn the Warrior Ethos:

I will always place the mission first.
I will never accept defeat.
I will never quit.
I will never leave a fallen comrade.

In addition, recruits must memorize—and take to heart— the Seven Core Army Values throughout the course. These are loyalty, duty, respect, selfless service, honor, integrity, and personal courage. For 10 weeks, recruits engage in physical and mental training. Weapons training and defense is a vital part of the basic combat training course. During the Red Phase, recruits learn to defend themselves against nuclear, biological, and chemical weapons. They learn to guard against land mines and other dangers. During the White Phase, recruits practice their rifle marksmanship. Finally, during the Blue Phase, recruits qualify on weapons such as machine guns and hand grenades.

\(\!\!\(\!\(\!\(\!\(\!\(\!\(\!\(\!\(\!\(\!\(\!\(\!\(\!\(\!\(\! ★ \)

Stephanie chambered another round and fired again.

Stephanie Lincoln was born on December 14, 1979. She describes herself as having been a bit of a tomboy and a daddy's girl. The oldest of four girls, she likes to think she was the son her father never had. She grew up mostly in Jacksonville, Florida, where she played softball and soccer, and spent plenty of time in the woods. She also loved to sew. In seventh grade, her grandma bought her a Singer sewing machine. Stephanie promptly began sewing cute pillows for all of her friends. At Sandalwood High School, once her sewing talent was discovered, she became the high school seamstress, repairing split pants and fixing torn football jerseys. Stephanie decided to go to fashion school as soon as she graduated.

One evening during her senior year, she was sitting at the dinner table with her parents and sisters. "I have news," she said. She told them about the acceptance letter she had received. She would start fashion school next fall.

No one said anything at first. Then her mother asked, "How will you pay for that?"

"Oh." *It costs money to go?* Stephanie had not realized she had to *pay* for college. She did know one thing, though: her parents did not have the money to send her.

"What about the military?" her dad interjected hopefully. Stephanie was no stranger to the military. Her dad was a 28-year navy and marines veteran, and she also had two uncles in the service. Even her grandfather had served. She had heard the story many times about how he had been injured on the beaches of Normandy during World War II.

"Okay," she said slowly. She sat up. *Yes,* she decided, *That IS what I want to do.*

Stephanie enlisted in the US National Guard a few months before graduating from high school. As a member of the guard, she would work part time for the army and still be able to attend school and work at a civilian job. She took the ASVAB, which she learned stood for Armed Services Vocational Aptitude Battery, the military entrance exam. She was hoping the test would qualify her for a MOS—military occupation specialty—having to do with clothing. Didn't soldiers need someone to design and maybe repair their uniforms?

She was assigned to a unit and would "drill" with them one weekend a month until she shipped to the basic combat training course next October. *What's drill?* she thought, *What do I do?* Luckily, there was an expert in the family. Stephanie went to talk to her dad.

"The first thing you need to do is shine your boots," she remembers him saying. The military, he explained, was all about discipline. And details. "Do everything 100 percent and even exceed the standard."

He turned on the TV, and he and Stephanie spent the next hour—hour!—shining her boots. Next he showed her how to iron her uniform, how to get the creases perfect. She was astounded that even her hat needed to be starched and ironed. They did this routine every day. When Stephanie reported for her first drill weekend, her attention to detail showed. She looked sharp! Not only that, some of the noncommissioned officers commented on her excellent discipline. She was all set for boot camp. Or so she thought.

Basic combat training—boot camp—was at Fort Jackson, South Carolina. Stephanie stepped off the bus. She looked around and tried to find someone she could connect with. She was 17 years old and had never been away from home for this long. A surge of homesickness hit her like a rogue wave at the beach. Who were these other people, strangers who seemed like they had nothing in common with her?

Stephanie Lincoln with gear.
Stephanie Lincoln

"Hurry up! Go, go, GO!" The drill sergeant roared at the recruits as they hustled from the bus carrying their gear. Stephanie had four sets of socks and underwear, a jacket, gloves, hats, and two pairs of boots. One set of boots had a dot on the back. To ensure even wear of both pairs, the dotted boots were for Mondays, Wednesdays, and Fridays. The unmarked boots were for the rest of the week. She had also been issued four uniforms—two lighter summer ones and two heavier winter versions. Both were basically comfortable but made from a stiff, camouflaged material.

Most days started at 4:00 AM, earlier if she had KP duty (kitchen patrol). Every couple of weeks when she was assigned to KP, she got up at 2:00 AM. She also had "fire watch." This was when two people had to guard the barracks at night, patrolling the area and making sure all cadets were accounted for. In the mornings, once up, she had five minutes—no more—to use the bathroom, brush her teeth, make her bed perfectly, and be ready in her PT (physical training) uniform. To save time, she learned to sleep fully dressed on top of her covers. That way, the hospital corners she had used to tuck in her bed sheets were not too messed up.

Physical training was tough. There was running, marching, endless sit-ups, and lots and lots of push-ups. Stephanie thought she was ready for this part of the course, but it still challenged her. Before enlisting, she had not done one push-up in her whole life—now she worked her way up to 25. She trained until she could do 50 sit-ups in two minutes. And the exercise was all outside, no matter how nasty the weather was. Once on an extended field exercise, the water in her canteen froze. *I will never accept defeat. I will never quit.* Stephanie repeated the Warrior Ethos over and over as she pushed her body further than she ever had before.

In addition to fieldwork, Stephanie absorbed classroom lessons on first aid, army traditions and values, and using basic military equipment like a radio or compass. She was informed of her first assignment, her MOS. She would go to AIT—Advanced Individual Training—to be a finance specialist. *Nothing to do with sewing, huh?*

In mid-December, near the end of the course, she told her drill sergeant that it was her 18th birthday.

"Then give me 18 push-ups!" he told her.

Finally, it was almost the end of the course. "I want you to compete for 'Best Soldier of the Cycle,'" her drill sergeant told her. Stephanie was shocked. It was a prestigious award, in fact, the highest award possible during basic training. Now the pressure was really on. She would go in front of a board of the toughest, most demanding instructors on base. They would grill her with questions and scrutinize how well she could perform certain tasks. And if she messed up . . . well, it would not be good.

Stephanie took a deep breath until, suddenly, she made up her mind. *I'm not going to stress about it. I'm just going to do it.* When it was her turn, she squared her shoulders and walked in.

"What's the millimeter of the M16A1 ammunition?" the first evaluator barked.

"How many moves does it take to break down your M16 to get to the firing pin?"

"What is the farthest firing range of a grenade launcher?"

Stephanie nailed every question and every task they threw at her. She won the contest. On graduation day, the general in charge spoke to her personally. She could barely believe it. A general was talking to *her*, congratulating her in front of everyone! She earned a special coin and got to march with that same general. It was a proud moment.

"You need to go to Officer Candidate School," several people told her. She had not really considered OCS, but then her dad said the same thing.

It was another two years, but then she did enroll in the school that changed enlisted soldiers into officers. Once there Stephanie found that OCS was *completely* different from boot camp. In basic training, the expectation was that you did not know anything—true. Now in OCS, the expectation was that she already knew everything—not true at all. Stephanie had to scramble to meet the standards.

There were over 40 people in Stephanie's OCS, including about 15 women (only 5 or 6 made it to the end). The course started in April 2001 and ended a year and a half later. It required one weekend every month, plus two stints of two weeks each. Stephanie was still able to attend college. By this time she was three-quarters of the way toward earning her bachelor's degree in psychology.

At first, the OCS classroom lessons focused on traditional army customs. The "pomp and circumstance" included how to set formal place settings and the correct protocol for a formal dinner. Then the unthinkable happened on September 11 and everything changed. Nineteen terrorists from the extremist group al-Qaeda (ahl-KAY-dah) attacked the United States. They used four airplanes with tanks full of fuel for a transcontinental flight to crash into various targets, killing thousands of people and wounding thousands more. A new commander took over Stephanie's battalion. The training now was all about combat readiness.

"You guys are going to war."

Graduation day was a proud but somber day for Stephanie. As an officer, Stephanie now had an incredible responsibility. When the ceremony was about to start, her family still was not in the audience. She had planned for her parents to pin on her "butterbars," the gold bar insignia for her newly earned rank of second lieutenant. Scanning the audience one more time, she asked her soon-to-be com-pany commander to do the honors instead.

The ceremony started. *There!* Her family had made it after all. When it was Steph-anie's turn to get pinned, she stood at attention. Her father came up wearing a set of brand new dress whites. (The reason he had been late, she learned later, was that he

Second Lieutenant Stephanie Lincoln's first salute to her father. *Stephanie Lincoln*

was purchasing this new uniform at the base store and had to get it to fit properly.) Following the appropriate army protocol, her dad rendered Stephanie's first salute. His daughter now out-ranked him. Stephanie could not have felt more proud.

Stephanie's unit was called to war a few months later. She initially thought she would go with them, but was disappointed to learn that she was disqualified from going. She needed to complete the mandatory officer's training course first. She was still able to serve stateside, thankfully. Promoted to executive

Captain Stephanie Lincoln. *Stephanie Lincoln*

officer, she was the second in command of the important rear detachment. She would be part of the smaller unit in the States that would support those over in the Middle East. During the tense years following the 9/11 attacks, Stephanie worked in the Signal Corps, the branch of the army in charge of communications. She later took a job as a drill instructor. Now it was her job to develop tough, resilient soldiers. She loved it.

In 2007 Stephanie's dad was diagnosed with cancer. She made a decision to resign from the army, though she did not get too far away from it. Equipped with an advanced degree in psychology now, she worked as a civilian, running a mental health program for the National Guard in Florida and later as deputy director of a similar program for the Air Guard. Today, Stephanie works at her own counseling business to promote wellness in service members. She works with current troops as well as veterans, knowing that her intervention will strengthen and empower people to reach their full potential.

"[The military] will be the most challenging thing you've ever done, but the best thing you've ever done." Stephanie's experience in the army changed her. She learned to be a very good follower, but also a good leader. Confident, strong, and fit, she says the army is what made her who she is today.

★ LEARN MORE ★

Becoming a Soldier—United States Army, www.goarmy.com /soldier-life/becoming-a-soldier.html

Undaunted: The Real Story of America's Servicewomen in Today's Military by Tanya Biank (New York, NY: NAL Caliber, 2013)

Leigh Ann Hester

Silver Performer

L eigh Ann Hester, a military police officer (MP) with the 617th from the Kentucky National Guard, was standing at attention. She was with five members of her squad and several steps ahead of the rest of the troops. Lieutenant General John R. Vines, commanding general of the Multi-National Corps—Iraq, strode across the gravel at Camp Liberty. He stashed his rifle underneath the podium that was set up for the occasion and straightened up. "Parade, REST," he ordered the soldiers.

As one, Leigh Ann and the others took a more relaxed stance, legs slightly apart and hands clasped at the small of their backs. The ceremony began.

"My heroes don't play in the NBA and don't play in the US Open at Pinehurst." The general paused to look over the troops. "They're standing in front of me today. These are American heroes."

Lt. General John R. Vines addresses soldiers at an awards ceremony at Camp Liberty, Iraq, June 16, 2005. Awardees, left to right, are: Staff Sgt. Timothy Nein, Sgt. Leigh Ann Hester, Spc. Jason Mike, Spc. Casey Cooper, Sgt. Dustin Morris, and Spc. Jesse Ordunez. *US Army photo by Spc. Jeremy D. Crisp*

Leigh Ann listened to the general, a sheen of sweat covering her face. It was hot, as usual. The temperature would climb to well over 100 degrees Fahrenheit today. *Well, it is June in Iraq,* Leigh Ann thought to herself. In fact, it was June 16, 2005, and she was at Camp Liberty, an American military base near the Baghdad airport in Iraq. To her right was her squad leader, Staff Sergeant (SSG) Timothy Nein. On her left was Specialist Jason Mike, the medic on the team. All three of them were receiving a Silver Star Medal today for their actions during an ambush by Anti-Iraq Forces (AIF) three months ago, on March 20. Next to Jason were three others from her squad. They would all get service recognition medals today as well.

General Vines started with Nein, attaching the star-shaped medal to the lapel of his left-side pocket. Nein stepped back into line, and Leigh Ann was next. She stepped forward and assumed a position of attention, making her petite, five-foot-four-inch frame as tall as possible. But tall or short, it didn't matter. The ceremony today made Leigh Ann feel 10 feet tall.

"For valor and extraordinary achievement during convoy operations in Baghdad, Iraq, on 20 March 2005 . . . Sergeant Hester's dedication to her fellow soldiers during battle upholds the finest traditions of military service." Leigh Ann resisted the urge to look at the medal now attached to *her* uniform. It was pretty cool to earn a medal in combat, though she still didn't realize just how significant the achievement really was. That would come later, with reporter after reporter calling for an interview and the US Army Women's Museum featuring her in a permanent exhibit. Things would get completely unbelievable when some toy company made an *action figure* of her.

Today, Leigh Ann was just glad she was doing her part in Operation Iraqi Freedom. She was thankful that no one on her team had died during the firefight three months ago, and she was looking forward to completing her mission.

Leigh Ann was born on January 12, 1982. She grew up in Bowling Green, Kentucky. She had an active childhood playing softball and basketball and spending time with her family. For as long as she could remember, Leigh Ann dreamed about being a police officer. She looked up to anybody in uniform, actually— soldiers or police—and was especially impressed when that person was female. Her role models were her uncle, Carl Sollinger, who served in Vietnam, and her grandfather, Oran Sollinger, who earned a Bronze Star in World War II.

After graduating from high school, Leigh Ann moved to Nashville, Tennessee, where she was the manager of a shoe

After receiving the Silver Star award, Sergeant Leigh Ann Hester stands at parade rest. Camp Liberty, Iraq, June 16, 2005. *US Army photo by Spc. Jeremy D. Crisp*

GALLANTRY IN ACTION—THE SILVER STAR

The Silver Star Medal is the third-highest military award given for heroism in combat. It comes after the Medal of Honor and the Distinguished Service Cross. The Silver Star is not unique to the army. Any of the service branches can bestow the award—the army, navy, marines, air force, coast guard, or merchant marines. The medal is also authorized for foreign allies or even civilians who have shown exceptional bravery in support of a US combat mission. When Leigh Ann earned the Silver Star, she was the first female to receive the honor since World War II. Over 60 years before, four army nurses were the first women to receive this rare and prestigious award. On February 10, 1944, led by Mary Roberts Wilson, these four army nurses evacuated 42 patients by flashlight from the 33rd Field Hospital in Anzio, Italy, while under heavy enemy fire. One woman, fatally wounded during the attack, received the award after her death. Leigh Ann was the first woman to receive the Silver Star Medal for combat action.

《《《《《《《《《《《《《《《《《《《《《 ★ 》》》》》》》》》》》》》》》》》》》》》

store. She was 19 in April 2001 when she joined the National Guard with the idea of being a military police officer. She signed all of the paperwork and waited for her orders to report to the basic training course. On September 11, 2001, terrorists hijacked four airplanes and crashed them into the twin towers of the World Trade Center in New York City and the Pentagon in Washington, DC. The fourth plane smashed into a field in Pennsylvania when passengers fought against the men who had taken over the plane. President George W. Bush later spoke to the nation from the White House. "Terrorist attacks can shake the foundations of our biggest buildings, but they cannot touch the foundation of America. These acts shatter steel, but they cannot dent the steel of American resolve."

The United States declared a war on terror.

When Leigh Ann entered basic training, her instructors prepared her class to support the United States' War on Terror. They predicted that she and the other recruits would deploy to

《《《《《《《《《《《《《《《《《《《《《《《《《《《《《 ★ 》》》》》》》》》》》》》》》》》》》》》》》》》》》》》

WAR ON TERROR

Immediately following the terror attacks on September 11, the United States and several allies initiated a military campaign in Afghanistan called Operation Enduring Freedom. They fought against the terrorist group al-Qaeda and its leader, Osama bin Laden. Al-Qaeda was the group responsible for the 9/11 attacks, and the leaders of Afghanistan—the Taliban—had allowed them to run training camps there. Soon after the military strikes against these camps, Iraq became the next target. Iraq's violent dictator, Saddam Hussein, was said to be sheltering terrorists as well as stockpiling weapons of mass destruction (WMDs) such as nuclear bombs and chemical or biological agents. These weapons were never found, but the invasion toppled Saddam's regime and paved the way for a new, democratic government. Named Operation Iraqi Freedom, the United States and Britain led the invasion into Iraq on March 20, 2003. Ten years after the events on 9/11, a team of US special forces located and killed Osama bin Laden in a guarded compound in Abbottabad, Pakistan, on May 2, 2011.

《《《《《《《《《《《《《《《《《《《《《《《《《《《《《 ★ 》》》》》》》》》》》》》》》》》》》》》》》》》》》》》

the Middle East soon. There was suddenly a very real threat to the security of people in the United States, and well-prepared soldiers were needed to fight against this danger. Instead of the usual once-a-month training, Leigh Ann's unit met for three- and four-day drills and then longer, two-week stretches. They trained for combat readiness.

In 2004 Leigh Ann packed her gear and headed to Iraq. She was now a sergeant and a member of the 617th Military Police Company out of Kentucky. Her job was well defined: "Our mission in Iraq was to clear the main supply routes and make sure that convoys and supplies got through our area of operation safely." Leigh Ann would drive on the supply route highways in a Humvee loaded with weapons, including a gun turret on top. Her team would provide security to the supply convoys in case of an ambush. They would also look for homemade bombs called Improvised Explosive Devices (IEDs) on or along the road.

Leigh Ann met a lot of people in Iraq, and while some were "bad guys," many others were not. One day her team stopped for a security halt. They waited while another squad investigated some suspicious trash by the side of the road—terrorists often disguised IEDs this way. While Leigh Ann waited, a couple of small heads popped over a stone wall in front of a house. It was a group of young children, curiosity overcoming their fear of the American soldiers. Leigh Ann waved them over. After a little coaxing, the children came near. One little girl carried a workbook for learning English. Leigh Ann pointed to one of the words in the workbook. "Cat," she said.

"Cat," the little girl answered.

Leigh Ann kept reading more of the words for the girl, who repeated each one eagerly. Finally, it was time to leave. As Leigh Ann turned to go, the girl thrust forward a simple homemade doll, a gift for the lady American soldier. Leigh Ann tucked the precious memento into her uniform, knowing she would never forget that sweet Iraqi girl.

Another day was not so poignant. This time, the daily routine turned deadly. It took skill—and certainly luck—to keep Leigh Ann and her team alive. March 20, 2005, was the day Leigh Ann earned her Silver Star. This was the day of the Palm Sunday Ambush.

The temperature that day was pleasant, a sunny 75 degrees. Leigh Ann's team, named Raven 42, was involved in their normal procedure of securing their assigned roads. In three Humvees, they had been up early and had driven through the area to check for IEDs and insurgents—rebel terrorists intent on inflicting harm. They had not encountered either. As usual, once the team declared the roads cleared, a convoy of various supply trucks began their daily travel along that route. Raven 42 would continue patrolling the highway to make sure the line of trucks moved safely through. The day would be anything but routine, however. In fact, Leigh Ann would have to fight for her and her teammates' lives.

The section of the highway where the ambush took place was near a place called Salman Pak, southeast of Baghdad. Raven 42 was trailing behind a convoy of about 30 tractor trailers with mostly Turkish-speaking drivers. They were a sustainment convoy, transporting food and other necessary supplies. On either side of the highway were irrigation ditches and patches of open desert dotted with scattered trees. In this particular area an orchard provided additional cover for the enemy.

The first sign of trouble was the rattle of nearby gunfire. The trucks ahead abruptly stopped. When Leigh Ann saw the smoke, she knew there was a serious problem. The lead vehicle in the convoy was on fire, and it blocked the others from moving past.

Unable to keep driving, the rest of the convoy was stuck in the kill zone—the area of most danger and where the AIF (Anti-Iraq Forces) were concentrating their attack.

Leigh Ann was in the passenger seat of the second Humvee when the Raven 42 squad sprang into action. All three vehicles drove between two of the marooned supply trucks and put themselves between the convoy and the bullets flying from the side of the road. As the Humvees sped along the shoulder of the road, gunners from the turrets on top of the vehicles fired into the trench and orchard while taking fire from the enemy. The squad leader, Staff Sergeant Timothy Nein, knew of a side access road. He led the other two vehicles to this road, intending to attack the insurgents from this vantage point.

Leigh Ann noted that seven vehicles were parked along this side road, each with all four doors and their trunks open. It was a chilling discovery. These were the getaway cars and the trunks were for taking prisoners. One more thing: if there were seven cars, that meant they were up against a large group of AIF, maybe 28 or more enemy forces. Raven 42 was a team of only nine soldiers, plus one medic. The enemy were attacking using AK-47s, RPK machine guns, and rocket-propelled grenades (RPGs). Raven 42 was the convoy's only defense.

Down the access road now, an RPG had hit the lead Humvee. The gunner, Casey Cooper, was momentarily knocked unconscious. Flanked along the access road, Leigh Ann could see a large number of enemy fighters lining the irrigation ditches and using the orchard's trees for cover. She realized there were a lot more than even 28 insurgents, but there was no time to think about how greatly outnumbered her team was. She exited her vehicle in front of the hail of bullets, and, with two others in the team, ducked behind an embankment. She began firing her weapon, an M203 grenade launcher.

Meanwhile, the last Humvee was caught in the worst of the firestorm. It was in trouble. Three of the four-person crew were wounded. The uninjured soldier, a medic named Mike, was left to defend them all until others could come and help.

Leigh Ann and Timothy Nein had their own focus. They needed to clear the area or else more civilians and service members were going to die. Leigh Ann's training kicked in. She did not stop to think of the danger, but rolled over the edge of the ditch with Timothy, carrying her M4 assault rifle. Inside the trench the ground was uneven. AIF fired at them and Leigh Ann fired back. "The adrenaline was pumping, the bullets were flying, and I didn't have any choice but to fight back."

When it was all over, 27 AIF were dead, 6 were wounded, and 1 was taken prisoner. Leigh Ann helped to collect the abandoned weapons: AK-47 assault rifles, RPG launchers and rockets, hand grenades, and stacks of ammunition. In addition, many of the AIF had handcuffs with them, another indication that they had planned to take prisoners during the well-planned assault. This had been no small operation. It was just another day for Leigh Ann Hester and her team.

In all, Leigh Ann completed three deployments to the Middle East, earning the rank of sergeant first class. Her two mobilizations to Afghanistan were back-to-back. Throughout her tours of duty, there were many difficult times, but thankfully nothing was as dangerous as the events on March 20 had been. When Leigh Ann finally moved back to her civilian life in Franklin, Tennessee, she got herself a puppy named Reno, and picked up where she left off. In between deployments, she had earned a place in the Franklin Police Department. She slipped back into her duties as a patrol officer after her colleagues, headed by Chief Deborah Faulkner, honored Leigh Ann with a welcome-back ceremony. "Being a police officer is rewarding, and I can't imagine doing anything other than being a soldier and a cop; I love both," she said to the crowd. "I'm glad to be home, and am honored to serve our country and Franklin." Yet, it was an adjustment to live as a civilian once again. It was especially difficult to sit still in traffic—in combat, soldiers were trained to never stop moving.

Leigh Ann received other recognition. In addition to the features in newspapers and media outlets all over the country, the US Army Women's Museum at Fort Lee, Virginia, built a permanent display highlighting the Raven 42 team's contributions to the War on Terror. At the unveiling ceremony, Leigh Ann said, "If you have a goal or a dream, you can do it. . . . If your heart is set on it, don't let anything stand in your way."

Today, Leigh Ann still works for the Franklin Police, but on June 9, 2017, the chief released an announcement: Leigh Ann had been promoted to detective. She says of her experience as a military police officer: "Twenty years ago, or thirty years ago, there weren't any women MPs, and now there's thousands. There are almost as many women MPs as there are men. . . . If you're capable, like I said, whether or not you're a man or a woman, if you're capable of doing the job, why shouldn't you be able to do that job."

★ LEARN MORE ★

United States Army Women's Museum, www.awm.lee.army.mil
Unsung Heroes: The Story of America's Female Patriots directed by
    Frank Martin (Agoura Hills, CA: Eleventh Day Entertainment, Workaholic Productions, 2014)

Deborah Kotulich

On the Shoulders of Giants

"**I**'m driving a tank. I'm actually driving a tank!"

These were the words Deb Kotulich whispered to herself as she dropped into the compartment of a M1 tank. She was surrounded by thick, cold steel and an array of complicated switches and equipment. She strapped herself in. Inside the tank there were no windows, and Deb knew she could easily feel claustrophobic or overwhelmed in this cramped space. The only view of the outside was through a driver's scope. She forced herself to power through, to focus on the mission. It was a combat simulation in which her team would shoot at real targets, but with laser beams instead of the tank's regular steel rounds.

"Tank 1, ready?" Deb called out.

"Roger," the team responded. There were three others: the gunner, driver, and loader. Deb was the tank commander. Now she peered through the driver's scope at the distorted landscape outside and told herself that this was just another vehicle, bigger than a car for sure, but still just a vehicle. Then they were driving. The tank was loud—and bumpy. They were driving cross-country through gullies and over embankments. It was nothing like driving her Saturn. This was intense. And it was fun.

"Fire!"

The laser equipment hit its mark. They fired again. Another point. They might just win this exercise!

Deb was 19 years old. She was a cadet at West Point, the US Military Academy, and it was 1987, a year after she had asked her guidance counselor at Bridgewater Raritan High School, "What's a military academy?" She had entered the academy with decent high school grades, a black belt in karate, and parents who were proud but knew nothing about the military. Deb had been just as clueless, but she was learning fast.

Next up was Jump School.

Airborne School—Jump School—was also intense. The first week of the three-week training was all groundwork. Deb worked alongside the others to increase her physical fitness, to understand her parachute, and to learn how to land. At first she was instructed to jump from a large box. The second week they moved up to jumping from a 200-foot tower wearing a harness. The training included getting in and out of an airplane. When it was time to practice with the real thing, they would be taking a C-130 Hercules, a large-bellied aircraft that could hold up to 64 paratroopers. In order to graduate, she would need to complete five jumps. Two of those would be with full combat gear, including a mock weapon. One would be at night.

Several questions ran through Deb's mind. *How do you avoid getting tangled? How do you avoid the other jumpers in the air? What if the parachute doesn't open?* Deb knew that falling at approximately 120 miles per hour, she could fall to her death if something went wrong. *Nothing's going to go wrong*, she told herself.

Finally, it was the third week of the course. Deb lined up on the tarmac with the others. "There's only one way you're going to come down," the instructor reminded them needlessly. Deb let the words sink in. She was either going to jump from that plane on her own—or get pushed.

She resisted the urge to check her equipment one more time; anyway, it was too late. It was her turn to step into the plane. Inside, she sat down and attached the safety harness. Minutes ticked by as the plane climbed to 800, then 1,250 feet in the air. *I can do this*, she reassured herself, but her palms were sweaty and she could hear her heart thumping double-time. She knew she had checked and rechecked everything. *I'm good to go.* She ran through a mental checklist:

Don't look down.

Look at the horizon.

Avoid the other jumpers.

Don't get tangled and fall to my death.

Really, don't look down.

They were standing up. In a couple of minutes, the team would exit the plane quickly, one after the other. Once in the air, the jump was going to be fast. "GO!" Deb was out of the plane and in the air. Her parachute streamed out behind her and opened. There was no time to think, only react as the horizon got higher and higher. *Don't look down.*

The ground rose up to meet her, and she angled her legs out in preparation to land. She felt the earth under her boots and completed a five-point roll landing. She had made it! Her first jump!

Deb Kotulich spent her childhood in Bridgewater, New Jersey. She was born on May 27, 1968, one year after her brother, Mark. Because of the gap in their ages, Deb was introduced to karate a year before she was allowed to participate. At the age

(((((((((((((((((((((((((((((((((((★))))))))))))))))))))))))))))))))))))

JUMP SCHOOL

The course to become qualified as a US paratrooper is officially known as Basic Airborne School (BAC). It is located
at Fort Benning, Georgia, and takes three weeks to complete. There are several requirements to qualify for the
course, including being able to pull yourself up on a chin-up
bar for a minimum of 20 seconds. The first week, Ground
Week, is when students practice various techniques like
proper exit from a mock airplane door and how to land from
a jump. Next is Tower Week, when students jump from a
250-foot tower. Last is Jump Week. Here students complete five jumps from a C-130 or C-17 plane at 1,250 feet.
Two of the jumps are with equipment. Three jumps, nicknamed "Hollywood," include only the jumper plus his or her
parachute and a reserve. One of these jumps is at night.
Successful graduates receive a Parachutist Badge (Jump
Wings). In 1973 Privates Rita Johnson and Janice Kutch
were the first females to graduate from the course.

(((((((((((((((((((((((((((((((((((★))))))))))))))))))))))))))))))))))))

of 9, she went every week to watch her brother's lesson. Deb
was dying to join in, but the karate instructor was insistent: no
students would be admitted until they were 10 years old. She
began karate lessons as soon as she could and earned a black belt
by the time she was 17.

Deb was active in other sports as well. She excelled at softball,
soccer, basketball, anything—she loved being athletic. Deb was
also a decent student, though she was not an avid reader until
she began reading stories about men and women role models.
She compared her life experience to that of Abraham Lincoln.

Despite his humble beginnings, he grew up to become president of the United States. President! Could Deb, too, do something important with her life?

Deb's family did not have a lot of money. They certainly could not afford to pay for college. Ambitious and bright, Deb was determined—there had to be a way to continue her education.

Then, Deb won a small athletic scholarship and was one step closer to accomplishing her goal. She looked into college tuition but realized that the scholarship was still not enough.

"I have no money. How can I go to college?" she asked her guidance counselor.

"You? *You* need a military academy."

Deb quickly learned what a military academy was. Yes! Why hadn't she known about this earlier? She applied to the military academies of the merchant marines, the navy, and the army. It was a two-pronged process. First she had to get a nomination. To attend a military academy, she needed to get a congressman, senator, or the vice president to nominate her. Then she had to be accepted. Deb secured the nomination, crossed her fingers, and completed the rest of the application forms. She dropped each of them into the mail. And waited.

Deb was accepted to West Point and graduated in 1990, 10 years after the first class of female cadets. She felt like she was standing on the shoulders of giants, men and women who had come before her, creating the gender-integrated army of today.

Deb was 22 years old and a second lieutenant when she got her first assignment as platoon leader. Fluent in German, she headed overseas to Kitzingen, Germany, to oversee a tank automotive unit. She enjoyed the mechanical aspect of the position. Her dad had been a heating and air-conditioning technician, and she had often watched him work. The noise and the tools of the shop were familiar, and she loved interacting with the soldiers.

(((((((((((((((((((((((((((((((((((★))))))))))))))))))))))))))))))))))))

DUTY, HONOR, COUNTRY

"To educate, train, and inspire the Corps of Cadets so that each graduate is a commissioned leader of character committed to the values of Duty, Honor, Country and prepared for a career of professional excellence and service to the nation as an officer in the United States Army."

This is the mission of the United States Military Academy at West Point, New York.

This army college is rich in history. George Washington, recognizing the strategic location of this western bank of the Hudson River, transferred his headquarters there in 1779. The college was founded on March 16, 1802. Now, the school serves as the United States' oldest continuously occupied military post. Although tuition is free for cadets, the competition to attend is fierce. Currently there are a little over 4,000 undergraduate students. Each had to pass rigorous tests for intelligence, fitness, and moral character. The first women were welcomed into the academy in 1976. In 1980 62 female cadets graduated as second lieutenants. Graduates of the academy devote a minimum of five years to active duty army service and an additional three years of Army Reserve service.

(((((((((((((((((((((((((((((((((((★))))))))))))))))))))))))))))))))))))

"What I liked was leading and caring for soldiers. They were all different backgrounds and education levels. Leading and caring for soldiers and their families."

Deb's three years in Germany coincided with the end of the Cold War. During her time there, she traveled to Berlin and saw both sides of the city that, up until 1989, had been separated by

Speaking with troops. *US Army photo by John Carkeet IV*

a guarded wall. She drove to the eastern side of the city. She
was not prepared for just how dramatic the difference was. The
roads were in poor repair and many buildings looked shabby
and run-down. There were no billboards or advertisements like
on the western side, and the shops carried little variety in goods.
Deb stopped and picked up a piece of the old Berlin wall. She
weighed the bit of broken concrete in her hand. *Incredible*, she
thought. *I am holding a piece of history*. The army, it turned out,
opened her eyes to things she had only ever heard or read about.
Deb felt a long way from Bridgewater, New Jersey.

Deb's next assignment was at Camp Casey in South Korea.
There she was a materiel management officer, in charge of main-
taining accountability and availability of weapons repair parts.
There was all sorts of equipment to support the engineers: combat earthmovers, tanks with spades to breach obstacles, army
vehicles and tools. Deb mused that she was responsible for

probably $30 million in repair parts. She strived to do the best job she could—and succeeded. Her company earned the best readiness rates. It was a busy time.

Life was about to get busier.

By the time she completed the Logistics Officer Advanced Course, Deb was now a captain. She asked to be compassionately reassigned. Her mother was ill, and Deb wanted to be closer to home to take care of her. She worked as a logistics

《《《《《《《《《《《《《《《《《《《《《《《《《《《《《《《《《《《《 ★ 》》》》》》》》》》》》》》》》》》》》》》》》》》》》》》》》》》》》》

THE BERLIN WALL AND THE COLD WAR

The Cold War was a period of tension between the Soviet Union and the United States. During World War II, France, Britain, America, and the Soviet Union worked together to defeat the Nazis in Germany. After the war, these allied countries each occupied a section of Berlin, the capital of Germany. As hostility between the Soviet Union and the other three countries escalated, soldiers from Soviet-occupied East Berlin built a wall to separate their portion of the city from the rest. Construction began on August 12, 1961, with over 30 miles of barbed wire fencing. A more permanent wall quickly followed. This wall, made of concrete, included 300 guard towers. Soldiers were ordered to shoot anyone who attempted to pass into the west. Nearly 200 people died trying to escape from East Berlin into the western portion of the city. But with the collapse of the Soviet Union, demolition of the wall began on November 9, 1989. People from all over the world scrambled to collect pieces of the wall, a physical reminder of this frightening period of history.

《《《《《《《《《《《《《《《《《《《《《《《《《《《《《《《《《《 ★ 》》》》》》》》》》》》》》》》》》》》》》》》》》》》》》》》》》》

officer and then an aide-de-camp for a major general, a Vietnam veteran whom she learned a lot from. She moved to Philadelphia, where her duties shrank to the needs of one person—the major general—but expanded to critical responsibilities she had never done before. Suddenly, there was little time for anything. Deb found herself supervising, managing, planning, and completing a wide variety of tasks. Though the motto was "mission first," the general reminded her, "Don't forget your family."

In 1997 Deb made a soul-searching decision. Her mother needed more care, and Deb decided to leave active duty. She planned to move her mother into her house where she could provide more help. Deb could not stay in the army and do both. It was the right thing to do, but the hardest thing to do. Maybe there was another way . . .

Deb did resign from active duty, but a few months later she signed up to be a "citizen soldier," a member of the US Army Reserve (USAR). If she joined the Reserve, she could stay in her house, take care of her mother, maintain her civilian job, and still be part of the army. It was perfect! In the Reserve, Deb quickly rose up the ranks. By 2001 she was promoted to major. Next she earned the rank of lieutenant colonel and then colonel. Finally, in 2016, she was promoted to brigadier general. About that same time, she was made partner of International Business Machines (IBM), her civilian job during her time in the Reserve.

Deb acknowledges that her life has been hectic, sometimes insanely so. However, balancing her military, civilian, and personal life was pretty doable, she says—until she made colonel. At IBM she was responsible for an enormous account, while simultaneously having to command a brigade of soldiers. Suddenly, one army weekend a month was not enough to get everything done. Then, 9/11 happened, and Deb deployed to the Middle East twice in support of Operation Iraqi Freedom

Brigadier General Deborah L. Kotulich, the Pentagon, Arlington, Virginia, August 10, 2016. *US Army photo by Monica King*

and Operation Enduring Freedom. Both times when she left her family behind, she felt torn. She knew she needed and wanted to serve her country, but she would also miss spending time with her wife and seeing her girls grow up. However, she says that in recent years the army has put a greater focus on support for families. One of the happiest moments of her life was during the change of command ceremony on July 23, 2016, when Deb took over command of the 143rd Expeditionary Sustainment Command (ESC). Her entire family was there to support her:

Brigadier General Deborah Kotulich (center), Colonel Timothy Bobroski (left), and Colonel Robert A. Wojciechowski (right) participate in a change of command ceremony, Fort Jackson, South Carolina, September 10, 2016. *US Army photo by SPC Jeff Russo*

her mother, brother, niece, two girls, her wife, and her wife's parents.

"The army gave me an education. It gave me leadership training and opportunities to achieve. . . . I owe everything I am today to the army. Everything I have today is because of the army."

★ LEARN MORE ★

Band of Sisters: American Women at War in Iraq by Kirsten Holmstedt (Mechanicsburg, PA: Stackpole Books, 2007)

Basic Airborne Course, United States Army, www.benning.army .mil/infantry/rtb/1-507th/airborne

United States Military Academy West Point, www.usma.edu /SitePages/Home.aspx

ACKNOWLEDGMENTS

Before I set out to write this book, I had given little thought to the evolution of women's participation in the army. It was only by studying the lives of these trailblazers that I began to grasp the enormous courage and heroic sacrifice each woman freely volunteered for this nation. I will be forever grateful to the women who shared their stories, both to me personally and by leaving behind a record of their accomplishments.

There was not enough space to include all the incredible women I spoke to while researching this book. In particular, my grateful thanks goes to Katherine Bissonette, Linda Carroll, Clara Chandler, Rhonda Humphrey, Julie Luckey, Nikki Olive, Kacey Rexing, Leah Rowell, and Miko Skerrett. My appreciation also extends to Carolyn Timbie, Grace Banker's granddaughter, and Jama Rattigan, who shared the story of her mother, Margaret KC Yang.

Many others volunteered their time and expertise to help me with this project. Ali Kolleda from the US Army Women's Museum and Britta Granrud from the Women in Military Service for America Memorial were especially helpful. Lieutenant Colonel Jay Billington from the Army Public Affairs office offered invaluable help. If I have left off others, please forgive me. This book would not have happened without the help of many generous people.

Next, a giant hug of gratitude goes to my critique partners: Laura Gehl, Hena Khan, Jenny Murray, and Joan Waites. Thank you, Kim Saphire and Barbara Schuler, for your encouragement. You are the best!

Lisa Reardon and Jerry Pohlen, thank you for taking a chance on an author you had not worked with before. Thank you to all the team at Chicago Review Press. You made the process comfortable and fun. I appreciate your incredible talent and expertise—it was a pleasure to work with you.

Finally, I truly thank my wonderful friends and family. My parents, Ruth and Helmut Klughammer, are the best anyone could hope for. My husband, Rich, is a blessing every day. My children are my joy and pride. Without your love and support, this book would never have happened.

GLOSSARY

Airborne School (Jump School): located at Fort Benning, Georgia, where service members train to become military parachutists

American Expeditionary Force (AEF): American soldiers who served in Europe during World War I

Armistice: an agreement signaling the end of World War I, signed on November 11, 1918

Army Reserve: a force of part-time soldiers who may be called to full-time status as needed

barracks: sleeping quarters for soldiers

basic training: the program of initial training to become a US soldier

battalion: a unit of several hundred soldiers, usually commanded by a lieutenant colonel

Buffalo Soldiers: African American soldiers serving on the western frontier of the United States in the years following the Civil War

camp followers: during the American Revolution, women who followed the soldiers from camp to camp to provide essential services such as cooking and laundry

Confederate army: the army of the Southern states during the US Civil War

Congressional Record: official notes of the happenings in the United States Congress

conscription: mandatory enlistment in the army

Continental army: army led by George Washington during the American Revolution

Direct Ground Combat Definition and Assignment Rule of 1994: law to define women's role in the army. In part, "Service members are eligible to be assigned to all positions for which they are qualified, except that women shall be excluded from assignment to units below the brigade level whose primary mission is to engage in direct combat on the ground"

Emancipation Proclamation: an executive order issued on January 1, 1863, by President Abraham Lincoln directing that all slaves within the United States be freed

infantry: foot soldiers within the army

insignia: an official badge to denote military rank

internment camps (relocation centers): camps set up to involuntarily house Japanese Americans after the 1942 bombing by the Japanese of Pearl Harbor, Hawai'i

mercenary: a professional soldier hired to serve in a foreign army

MOS: military occupational specialty

noncommissioned officer: an officer who has been promoted from the lowest, enlisted ranks instead of earning a direct appointment

Quartermaster Corps: the army branch in charge of logistics such as supplying food and equipment and other field services

Signal Corps: the army branch that directs all communication and information systems

Thirteenth Amendment to the US Constitution: a law passed by the Senate on April 8, 1864, and by the House on January 31, 1865, making slavery illegal

Union army: the army of the North during the American Civil War

Women's Armed Forces Integration Act: signed on June 12, 1948, a law declaring women permanent and regular members of the US Armed Forces

NOTES

Introduction

"There will be no . . . those who serve": Ash Carter, "Department of Defense Press Briefing by Secretary Carter in the Pentagon Briefing Room," December 3, 2015, https://dod.defense.gov/News/Transcripts/Transcript-View/Article/632578/department-of-defense-press-briefing-by-secretary-carter-in-the-pentagon-briefi.

"They'll be allowed": Carter, "Department of Defense Press Briefing."

"You have given up": Oveta Culp Hobby, "Greetings to Officer Candidates," July 23, 1942, speech transcript, Oveta Culp Hobby Papers, box 43, folder 15, Woodson Research Center, Rice University, Houston, Texas.

"Courage is more exhilarating": Eleanor Roosevelt, *You Learn by Living: Eleven Keys for a More Fulfilling Life* (New York: HarperCollins, 2011), 41.

Part I: Early America

"Their enlistment was prompted": "Female Soldiers: Two Women Discovered in the Union Uniform," *New York Times*, August 26, 1864.

"A woman's waist": Loreta Janeta Velazquez, *The Woman in Battle: The Civil War Narrative of Loreta Janeta Velazquez, Cuban Woman and Confederate Soldier* (Madison: University of Wisconsin Press, 2003), 58.

"A married woman named Clayton": "Another Female Soldier," *St. Paul Pioneer*, February 19, 1865.

Margaret Cochran Corbin: Ready, Aim!

"relieve her present necessities": Minutes of the Supreme Executive Council of Pennsylvania, Supreme Executive Council, Harrisburg, Pennsylvania, printed by T. Fenn, 1852–53, 34, https://babel.hathitrust.org/cgi/pt?id=hvd.32044032309734;view=1up;seq=54.

"that the case of": Minutes of the Supreme Executive Council of Pennsylvania, 34–35.

"Perhaps it would not": Fairfax Downey, "The Girls Behind the Guns," *American Heritage Magazine* 8, no. 1 (December 1956): 48.

IN APPRECIATION OF HER DEEDS: Grave memorial at the United States Military Academy at West Point.

Sarah Rosetta Wakeman: A Private Volunteer

"Have you a husband": Annie Wittenmyer, *Under the Guns: A Woman's Reminiscences of the Civil War* (Boston: E. B. Stillings, 1895), 18.

"I got when I enlisted": Sarah Rosetta Wakeman, *An Uncommon Soldier: The Civil War Letters of Sarah Rosetta Wakeman, Alias Pvt. Lyons Wakeman, 153rd Regiment, New York State Volunteers, 1862–1864*, ed. Lauren Cook Burgess (New York: Oxford University Press, 1995), 21.

"awatching for the rebels . . . If they do": Wakeman, *An Uncommon Soldier*, 36.

"first rate": Wakeman, *An Uncommon Soldier*, 28.

"getting fat as a hog": Wakeman, *An Uncommon Soldier*, 27.

"If I ever own a farm": Wakeman, *An Uncommon Soldier*, 31.

"I believe that God": Wakeman, *An Uncommon Soldier*, 25.

"I will help you": Wakeman, *An Uncommon Soldier*, 31.

"One of them was a Major": Wakeman, *An Uncommon Soldier*, 44.

"He who would be no slave": Abraham Lincoln to Henry L. Pierce and others, April 6, 1859, Abraham Lincoln Online, accessed October 31, 2017, www.abrahamlincolnonline.org/lincoln/speeches/pierce.htm.

"Neither slavery nor involuntary servitude": Article XIII, 38th Congress. (1865).

Cathay Williams: Buffalo Woman

"*I wanted to make my*": "She Fought Nobly: The Story of a Colored Heroine Who Served as a Regularly Enlisted Soldier During the Late War," *St. Louis Daily Times*, January 2, 1876.

"*free from all bodily defects*": Army enlistment certificate for William Cathay, St. Louis, Missouri, November 15, 1866, National Park Service, www.nps.gov/goga/learn/education/upload/BS_Primary Sources_2008-01-18_med.pdf.

"*I, William Cathay, do*": Army enlistment certificate for William Cathay.

"*And by virtue of the power*": Emancipation Proclamation, transcript, January 1, 1863, National Archives, www.archives.gov/exhibits /featured-documents/emancipation-proclamation/transcript.html.

a cousin and a "particular friend": "She Fought Nobly," *St. Louis Daily Times*.

"*He is unable to do military duty*": Army of the United States Certificate of Disability for Discharge, October 14, 1868, National Archives, www.nps.gov/goga/learn/education/upload/BS_Primary Sources_2008-01-18_med.pdf.

"*real bad*": "She Fought Nobly," *St. Louis Daily Times*.

"*was of no account*": "She Fought Nobly," *St. Louis Daily Times*.

Part II: The World at War

RESOURCEFUL, VERSATILE, AND SPEEDY RECRUITS: "American Girls as Linguists Operate Telephones in War," *Washington, DC, Evening Star*, May 19, 1918.

"*I do hereby establish a Women's*": Franklin D. Roosevelt, "Executive Order 9163 Establishing the Women's Army Auxiliary Corps," May 15, 1942, online by Gerhard Peters and John T. Woolley, American Presidency Project, www.presidency.ucsb.edu/ws/?pid=16256.

Grace Banker: Number, Please

"*Dear Sir . . . In the New York Globe*": Grace Banker, personal letter, December 9, 1917, private collection.

"*We are well in to*": Grace Banker, "Signal Corps Days in the A.E.F.," personal diary, 1918–1919, March 16, 1918, private collection.

"They look like a lot of skating": Banker diary, March 16, 1918.

At least it was something hot: Banker diary, March 17, 1918.

"When a line signal . . . Where directories . . . Conversation . . . if no answer": Military telephone regulations, section 4, September 1, 1918, 1–2, Army Women's Museum, Fort Lee, Virginia (hereafter referred to as "Army Women's Museum").

"Are you American . . . when you said": Banker diary, March 27, 1918.

"We are told to keep": Banker diary, May 20, 1918.

"All night long the streets": Grace Banker, "I Was a Hello Girl," *Yankee Magazine*, March 1974, 71.

"flimsy wood affairs": Banker diary, September 20, 1918.

"They tramp past our open door": Banker diary, September 28, 1918.

"Would you like to see": Dialogue adapted from Banker diary, 70.

War is hell: Banker diary, October 3, 1918.

Friday . . . When I get home: Banker diary, October 11–13, 1918.

"Hello boys!": Elizabeth Cobbs, *The Hello Girls: America's First Women Soldiers* (Cambridge, MA: Harvard University Press, 2017), 201.

"I could jump up": Banker diary, November 10, 1918.

Oveta Culp Hobby: The Little Colonel

"Your graduation today, in a real sense": Oveta Culp Hobby, "Address to Graduating Class of First Officers Candidate School," Fort Des Moines, Iowa, August 29, 1942, Hobby Speech, First OCS, 1942, B199-1, box 199, folder 1, Army Women's Museum.

"embarrassing the War": Mattie E. Treadwell, *United States Army in World War II: The Women's Army Corps* (Washington, DC: Center of Military History, United States Army, 1991), 13–15.

"Wackies . . . Petticoat Army": Mattie E. Treadwell, *United States Army in World War II: The Women's Army Corps* (Washington, DC: Center of Military History, United States Army, 1991), 49.

"serious menace to the home": James E. Cassidy, quoted in "Hobby's Army," Army & Navy, *Time*, January 17, 1944, 60.

"This is only the beginning": George C. Marshall, telegram to Oveta Culp Hobby, Fort Des Moines, Iowa, 1942, Hobby Speech, First OCS, 1942, B199-1, box 199, folder 1, Army Women's Museum.

"You might as well put my": Debra L. Winegarten, *Oveta Culp Hobby: Colonel, Cabinet Member, Philanthropist* (Austin: University of Texas Press, 2014), 5.

"Women will be selected": "To Lead Women," *Kansas City Star*, May 16, 1942.

"Even if Oveta Culp Hobby": "Hobby's Army," *Time*, 61.

"Leading ladies, but no prima donnas . . . Enrollment in the Corps": Oveta Culp Hobby, "The Role of Our Federal Government," speech at Howard University, Washington, DC, July 6, 1942.

Discussion of uniform: Treadwell, *Women's Army Corps*, 36–38.

"Behavior was average young female": "Hobby's Army," *Time*, 58.

"We're the Women of this Nation": Ruby Jane Douglass, "WAAC Parodies, Ruby Jane Douglass, 1943, B421," WAAC Publications Office, Fort Des Moines, Iowa, Army Women's Museum.

Statistics of WAC: Treadwell, *Women's Army Corps*, 765.

"We are earnestly determined": Hobby, "Role of Our Federal Government."

Charity Adams Earley: Letters from Home

"While we don't anticipate: Charity Adams Earley describes this scene in her book *One Woman's Army: A Black Officer Remembers the WAC* (College Station: Texas A & M University Press, 1989), 129.

"This is to certify that": Adams Earley, Orders for Active Duty, January 25, 1945, *One Women's Army*, 135.

"My brother and I": Adams Earley, *One Woman's Army*, 5.

"just work your mouth": Adams Earley, *One Woman's Army*, 9.

"Call home immediately": Adams Earley, *One Woman's Army*, 10. The dialogue that follows was adapted from pages 10–11 of *One Woman's Army*.

"I, a Negro, had my picture": Adams Earley, *One Woman's Army*, 16.

"Will all the colored girls": Adams Earley, *One Woman's Army*, 19.

"I do hereby establish": Roosevelt, "Executive Order 9163."

"We worked hard": Adams Earley, *One Woman's Army*, 83.

"How would you like": Adams Earley, *One Woman's Army*, 121.

No men Mondays: Adams Earley, *One Woman's Army*, 176.

"I have opened a few doors": Adams Earley, *One Woman's Army*, 214.

Margaret KC Yang: Pearl of Oʻahu

WAR! OAHU BOMBED: *Honolulu Star-Bulletin* 1st Extra, December 7, 1941.
"Citizens are urged to remain calm": NBCR KGU Honolulu Report radio broadcast, December 7, 1941, https://archive.org/details/1941 RadioNews/1941-12-07-1609-NBCR-KGU-Honolulu-Report.mp3.
"From now on": Honolulu Police Radio Broadcast log, December 1941, www.ibiblio.org/hyperwar/USA/USA-WH-Guard/USA-WH -Guard-8.html.
"Wave after wave of bombers": "War! Oahu Bombed," *Honolulu Star-Bulletin*.
"a respectable thing": Margaret KC Yang, "Chronology - WAC Travel," 1945, private collection.
"The following named enlisted": Yang Orders for Active Duty, Head-quarters Central Pacific Base Command. December 18, 1944, private collection.
Seating on the bus: Margaret KC Yang, "Chronology - WAC Travel," 1945, private collection.
"To you who answered the call": Harry Truman to Margaret KC Yang, June 27, 1946, private collection.
"W-A-C, W-A-C, Women's Army Corps": Eunice Kapuniai, "Hawaii's WAC, Carrying Ukes, Head 'Overseas' for Mainland," *Honolulu Advertiser*, January 12, 1945.

Elizabeth P. Hoisington: Good Old Army

"vividly remembers": Quentin Schillare, "Aunt Elizabeth: The Kansas Brat Who Became a Brigadier General," undated, private collection.
"a true supporter . . . always Army": Hickman Lione, "New WAC Chief from Baltimore," *Sun Magazine*, October 30, 1966, 4–6.
"All she had to hear": Joe Lastelic, "Army Not Strange to Colonel Hoisington: Kansas Daughter Is Top WAC," *Kansas City Star*, August 24, 1966.
"She said if she had learned": Matt Schudel, "Pioneering Brig. Gen. Elizabeth P. Hoisington," *Washington Post*, August 24, 2007.
"WAC personnel prepare": Anna W. Wilson, "The WAC: The Story of the WAC in the ETO," Lone Sentry, www.lonesentry.com/gi_stories _booklets/wac/wac.html.

"For meritorious service": Citation, Bronze Star, Elizabeth P. Hoisington, Army Women's Museum.

"taste just a little better": Stephanie Butler, "D-Day Rations: How Chocolate Helped Win the War," History, June 6, 2014, www.history.com/news/d-day-rations-how-chocolate-helped-win-the-war.

"Colonel Hoisington may yet": Lione, "New WAC Chief."

"Pallas Athene is shining": Elizabeth P. Hoisington, promotion ceremony, June 1970, "First Lady Generals," YouTube video, posted by "U.S. Army Women's Museum," June 9, 2017, www.youtube.com/watch?v=Zbf13Vu0Cvc.

Celia Adolphi: Farm Girl to Major General

"Welcome to our Home": Celia Adolphi, interview with the author, May 13, 2017.

FIRST FEMALE RESERVE: *Pentagram* (publication of the Department of Defense), November 5, 1999.

ARMY RESERVE GETS: Randy Pullen, USAWC alumni newsletter, November 29, 1999.

ARMY RESERVE HAS RICH HISTORY: *Army Times*, May 1, 2000.

FIRST FEMALE 2-STAR GENERAL: Curt Slyder, "First Female 2-Star General," *Enterprise*, date unknown.

"They [military women] have really been": Celia Adolphi, interview with Steven Green, Senior Officer Oral History Program, Project 2003–6, 87, http://usahec.contentdm.oclc.org/cdm/ref/collection/p16635coll26/id/96.

"The camaraderie with mission": Celia Adolphi, interview with the author, May 13, 2017.

LeAnn Swieczkowski: Petite and Powerful

"Come on, Ski": LeAnn Swieczkowski, interview with the author, July 17, 2017.

"Since entering the military": James Brown, "Pentagon Soldier Picture of Fitness," *Pentagram*, November 24, 1995.

We protect our country: LeAnn Swieczkowski, interview with the author, July 17, 2017.

"Hey, Ski!": LeAnn Swieczkowski, interview with the author, July 17, 2017.

"When you go": Dialogue from Swieczkowski interview.
"Another major benefit": LeAnn Swieczkowski, personal correspondence, July 4, 1993.
"But folks tell me I'm strong": Swieczkowski, personal correspondence, July 4, 1993.

Part IV: Current Conflicts

"Service members are eligible": Memorandum from Secretary of Defense Les Aspin, "Direct Ground Combat Definition and Assignment Rule," January 13, 1994, www.govexec.com/pdfs/031910d1.pdf.
"You don't really have time": Leigh Ann Hester, "Sergeant Hester and Captain Lindner," CBS interview, March 20, 2005, www.dvidshub .net/video/2056/sgt-hester-and-capt-lindner-cbs.
"In the 21st century": Matthew Rosenberg and Dave Philipps, "All Combat Roles Now Open to Women, Defense Secretary Says," *New York Times*, December 3, 2015.

Mary Hostetler: Citizen Soldier—Rock Steady

"There is nothing more awe inspiring": Jimmy Panetta, US Congressional Record, "In Honor of Chief Warrant Officer Five Mary A. Hostetler," 115th Congress, 1st session.
"The best thing I have ever done": Mary A. Hostetler, "Living the Dream: The Career of Chief Warrant Officer 5 Mary A. Hostetler," *Warrior Citizen: US Army Reserve Magazine*, 2017, 9.
"We've never had such": Mary Hostetler, interview with author, October 2017.
Being a special agent: Hostetler, interview with author, October 2017.
Challenges can defeat you: Hostetler, interview with author, October 2017.
"There will be challenges": Hostetler, interview with author, October 2017.

Stephanie Lincoln: Pretty Good at This Army Thing

"I will always place the mission first": United States Army Warrior Ethos, www.army.mil/article/50082/warrior_ethos.
"I have news": Dialogue from Stephanie Lincoln, interview with author, March 27, 2017.

"The first thing you need": Lincoln, interview with author, March 27, 2017.

"Then give me" and *"I want you to compete"*: Lincoln, interview with author, March 27, 2017.

"What's the millimeter": Lincoln, interview with author, March 27, 2017.

"You guys are going to war": Lincoln, interview with author, March 27, 2017.

"[The military] will be the most challenging": Lincoln, interview with author, March 27, 2017.

Leigh Ann Hester: Silver Performer

"My heroes don't play": Lt. General John R. Vines, speech at Camp Liberty, Iraq, June 16, 2005.

"For valor and extraordinary achievement": US Army award of the Silver Star to Leigh Ann Hester, Hall of Valor Project, https://valor.militarytimes.com/hero/3885.

"Terrorist attacks can shake": George W. Bush, "9/11 Address to the Nation," delivered September 11, 2001, Oval Office, Washington, DC.

"Our mission in Iraq" and *"bad guys"*: Interview with Leigh Ann Hester, November 16, 2012, *Unsung Heroes: The Story of America's Female Patriots*, directed by Frank Martin (Agoura Hills, CA: Eleventh Day Entertainment, Workaholic Productions, 2014).

"The adrenaline was pumping": Martin K. A. Morgan, "Sgt. Leigh Ann Hester, Raven-42 & the Silver Star," *American Rifleman*, July 3, 2013, www.americanrifleman.org/articles/2013/7/3/sgt-leigh-ann-hester-raven-42-the-silver-star.

"Being a police officer is rewarding": "Blue Star Flag Lowered as FPD Welcomes One of Their Own, Home," *City of Franklin, TN Police Department News*, August 20, 2015, www.franklintn.gov/Home/Components/News/News/3156/1082.

"If you have a goal or a dream": Kentucky National Guard, "New Women's Museum Exhibit Features Kentucky National Guard Sergeant," US Army website, February 5, 2007, www.army.mil/article/1689/new_womens_museum_exhibit_features_kentucky_national_guard_sergeant.

"Twenty years ago": Hester interview, *Unsung Heroes*.

Deborah Kotulich: On the Shoulders of Giants

"I'm driving a tank": Deborah Kotulich, interview with author, March 19, 2017.

"There's only one way": Kotulich, interview with author, March 19, 2017.

"Don't look down": Kotulich, interview with author, March 19, 2017.

"I have no money": Dialogue from Kotulich interview, March 19, 2017.

"To educate, train, and inspire": "Welcome to the United States Military Academy," United States Military Academy West Point, www.usma.edu/SitePages/Home.aspx.

"What I liked was leading": Kotulich, interview with author, March 19, 2017.

"The army gave me": Kotulich, interview with the author, March 19, 2017.

BIBLIOGRAPHY

Selected Books

Adams Earley, Charity. *One Woman's Army: A Black Officer Remembers the WAC*. College Station: Texas A & M University Press, 1989.

Atwood, Kathryn J. *Women Heroes of World War I: 16 Remarkable Resisters, Soldiers, Spies, and Medics*. Chicago: Chicago Review Press, 2016.

Atwood, Kathryn J. *Women Heroes of World War II: 26 Stories of Espionage, Sabotage, Resistance, and Rescue*. Chicago: Chicago Review Press, 2013.

Biank, Tanya. *Undaunted: The Real Story of America's Servicewomen in Today's Military*. New York: NAL Caliber, 2013.

Blanton, DeAnne, and Lauren M. Cook. *They Fought Like Demons: Women Soldiers in the American Civil War*. New York: Vintage Books, 2003.

Bremer, L. Paul, III. *My Year in Iraq: The Struggle to Build a Future of Hope*. New York: Simon and Schuster, 2006.

Brokaw, Tom. *The Greatest Generation*. New York: Random House, Paw Prints (imprint of Baker & Taylor Books), 2010.

Bugbee, Sylvia, ed. *An Officer and a Lady: The World War II Letters of Lt. Col. Betty Bandel, Women's Army Corps*. Lebanon, NH: University Press of New England in assoc. with the Military Women's Press of the Women in Military Service for America Memorial Foundation, 2004.

Casey, Susan. *Women Heroes of the American Revolution: 20 Stories of Espionage, Sabotage, Defiance, and Rescue.* Chicago: Chicago Review Press, 2017.

Cobbs, Elizabeth. *The Hello Girls: America's First Women Soldiers.* Cambridge, MA: Harvard University Press, 2017.

Cordell, M. R. *Courageous Women of the Civil War: Soldiers, Spies, Medics, and More.* Chicago: Chicago Review Press, 2016.

Davis, Burke. *The Civil War: Strange and Fascinating Facts.* New York: Fairfax, 1982.

Gavin, Lettie. *American Women in World War I: They Also Served.* Niwot: University Press of Colorado, 1997.

Hagerman, Keppel. *Dearest of Captains: A Biography of Sally Louisa Tompkins.* White Stone, VA: Brandylane, 1996.

Hall, Richard. *Patriots in Disguise: Women Warriors of the Civil War.* New York: Marlowe, 1994.

Hollihan, Kerrie L. *Reporting Under Fire: 16 Daring Women War Correspondents and Photojournalists.* Chicago: Chicago Review Press, 2014.

Holmstedt, Kirsten A. *Band of Sisters: American Women at War in Iraq.* Mechanicsburg, PA: Stackpole Books, 2007.

Lavine, A. Lincoln. *Circuits of Victory.* Garden City, NY: Doubleday, Page, 1921.

Leonard, Elizabeth D. *All the Daring of the Soldier: Women of the Civil War Armies.* New York: Penguin Books, 2001.

McDonald, Cornelia Peake. *A Woman's Civil War: A Diary with Reminiscences of the War, from March 1862.* Edited by Minrose C. Gwin. New York: Gramercy Books, 1992.

Moore, Brenda L. *To Serve My Country, to Serve My Race: The Story of the Only African American WACs Stationed Overseas During World War II.* New York: New York University Press, 1996.

Morden, Bettie J. *The Women's Army Corps 1945–1978.* Washington, DC: Center of Military History, United States Army, 1990.

Panchyk, Richard. *World War II for Kids: A History with 21 Activities.* Chicago: Chicago Review Press, 2002.

Roosevelt, Eleanor. *You Learn by Living: Eleven Keys for a More Fulfilling Life.* New York: HarperCollins, 2011.

Silcox-Jarrett, Diane, and Art Seiden. *Heroines of the American Revolution: America's Founding Mothers.* New York: Scholastic, 2000.

Treadwell, Mattie E. *United States Army in World War II: The Women's Army Corps.* Washington, DC: Center of Military History, United States Army, 1991.

Tsui, Bonnie. *She Went to the Field: Women Soldiers of the Civil War.* Guilford, CT: TwoDot, 2006.

Tucker, Phillip Thomas. *Cathy Williams: From Slave to Buffalo Soldier.* Mechanicsburg, PA: Stackpole Books, 2009.

Velazquez, Loreta Janeta. *The Woman in Battle: The Civil War Narrative of Loreta Janeta Velazquez, Cuban Woman and Confederate Soldier.* Madison: University of Wisconsin Press, 2003.

Wagner, Margaret E. *The Library of Congress Illustrated Timeline of the Civil War.* Boston: Little, Brown, 2011.

Wakeman, Sarah Rosetta. *An Uncommon Soldier: The Civil War Letters of Sarah Rosetta Wakeman, Alias Pvt. Lyons Wakeman, 153rd Regiment, New York State Volunteers, 1862–1864.* Edited by Lauren Cook Burgess. New York: Oxford University Press, 1995.

Winegarten, Debra L. *Oveta Culp Hobby: Colonel, Cabinet Member, Philanthropist.* Austin: University of Texas Press, 2014.

Wise, James E., and Scott Baron. *Women at War: Iraq, Afghanistan, and Other Conflicts.* Annapolis, MD: Naval Institute Press, 2011.

Wittenmyer, Annie. *Under the Guns: A Woman's Reminiscences of the Civil War.* Boston: E. B. Stillings, 1895.

Yellin, Emily. *Our Mothers' War: American Women at Home and at the Front During World War II.* New York: Free Press, 2005.

First Interviews with Author

Adolphi, Celia, May 13, 2017.
Hostetler, Mary, October 22, 2017.
Kotulich, Deborah, March 19, 2017.
Lincoln, Stephanie, March 27, 2017.
Rattigan, Jama, July 26, 2017.
Skerrett (Booth), Miko, February 24, 2017.
Swieczkowski, LeAnn, July 17, 2017.

Selected Articles, Newspapers, Other

Banker, Grace. "Signal Corps Days in the A.E.F." Personal Diary. 1918–1919.

Banker (Paddock), Grace. "I Was a Hello Girl." *Yankee Magazine,* March 1974.

Blanton, DeAnne. "Cathay Williams: Black Woman Soldier 1866–1868." *Minerva: Quarterly Report on Women and the Military* 10, nos. 3 & 4 (Fall 1992): 1–12.

"Blue Star Flag Lowered as FPD Welcomes One of Their Own, Home." *City of Franklin, TN Police Department News,* August 20, 2015. www .franklintn.gov/Home/Components/News/News/3156/1082.

Downey, Fairfax. "The Girls Behind the Guns." *American Heritage Magazine* 8, no. 1 (December 1956): 46–48.

Emancipation Proclamation, transcript. January 1, 1863. National Archives. https://www.archives.gov/exhibits/featured-documents /emancipation-proclamation/transcript.html.

Honolulu Police Radio Broadcast log, December 1941. In USAFMID-PAC Hist, Bulky File, backing papers to pt. 1, ch. 3.

Honolulu Star-Bulletin 1st Extra. "War! Oahu Bombed by Japanese Planes." December 7, 1941.

Kansas City Star. "To Lead Women." May 16, 1942.

Lastelic, Joe. "Army Not Strange to Colonel Hoisington: Kansas Daughter Is Top WAC." *Kansas City Star,* August 24, 1966.

Lincoln, Abraham, to Henry L. Pierce and others. April 6, 1859. Abraham Lincoln Online. Accessed October 31, 2017. www.abraham lincolnonline.org/lincoln/speeches/pierce.htm.

Minutes of the Supreme Executive Council of Pennsylvania. Supreme Executive Council, Harrisburg, Pennsylvania. Printed by T. Fenn, 1852–53. https://babel.hathitrust.org/cgi/pt?id=hvd.32044032309734;view=1up;seq=54.

Morgan, Martin K. A. "Sgt. Leigh Ann Hester, Raven-42 & the Silver Star." *American Rifleman,* July 3, 2013.

New York Times. "Female Soldiers: Two Women Discovered in the Union Uniform." August 26, 1864.

Roosevelt, Franklin D. "Executive Order 9163 Establishing the Women's Army Auxiliary Corps." May 15, 1942. Online by Gerhard Peters and John T. Woolley, American Presidency Project. www.presidency.ucsb.edu/node/210595.

Schudel, Matt. "Pioneering Brig. Gen. Elizabeth P. Hoisington." *Washington Post*, August 24, 2007.

St. Louis Daily Times. "She Fought Nobly: The Story of a Colored Heroine Who Served as a Regularly Enlisted Soldier During the Late War." January 2, 1876.

St. Paul Pioneer. "Another Female Soldier." February 19, 1865.

INDEX

Page numbers in italics refer to images.

abolitionists, 23
Adams, Charity. *See* Earley, Charity Adams
Adolphi, Celia, 115–125, *116, 117, 121*
  army firsts achieved by, 118–119
  awards and recognitions received by, 124
  background, 115–116
  as citizen soldier, 116–122
  education, 116
  postservice life, 124
  promotions of, 102, 117, 119, 122–124
African Americans
  Civil War service of, 22, 23, *33*
  as commissioned officers, 43, 66, 77, 79

discrimination against, 28, 43, 75
  segregation of, in army, 78
  in US Regular Army, 27, 28, 31
  See also Buffalo Soldiers
Airborne School. *See* Basic Airborne School
Allied forces, 83
al-Qaeda, 165, 173
American Civil War. *See* Civil War (1861–1865)
American Expeditionary Force (AEF), 39
American Revolution, 1, 8, 9, 12
Armistice, 55–56
Army Nurse Corps, 41
Army Reserve. *See* US Army Reserve (USAR)
Army's Physical Fitness Test (APFT), 127
Axis forces, 83

Baghdad, Iraq, 154, 155
Banker, Grace, 44–57, *45*, *56*
    awards received, 56
    background, 46
    as Hello Girl, 44–46, 47–56
    postservice life, 56–57
Barnes, Arie, *121*
Barracks Number Eight,
    Souilly, France, 53
Basic Airborne School (BAC),
    132, 180, 182
Basic Initial Entry Training Test
    (BIET), 149
basic training, 94–95, 128–129,
    130, 131–132, *132*, 159, 163
Battle of Berlin, 83
Battle of Fort Washington, 11
Battle of Normandy, 105
Battle of Pleasant Hill, 24
Battle of Saint-Mihiel, 52
Battle of the Bulge, 83
Beattie, Roxanna, *121*
Benson, Betty J., *113*
Berlin Wall, 184–185, *186*
Bigham, Samuel, 8
bin Laden, Osama, 173
Bonaparte, Napoleon, 123
boot camps. *See* basic training
Bray, Linda, 151
Bremer, L. Paul, III, 154
Buffalo Soldiers, 28, 34

C rations, 108, 111
C-54 cargo planes, 72
camp followers
    during American Revolu-
        tion, 8
    during Civil War, 27–29,
        33–34
Campbell, Abbie Noel, 72, 79, *81*
Campbell, Terry, *121*
cannons, firing of, 10
Captain Molly. *See* Corbin, Mar-
    garet Cochran
Carroll Prison, Washington,
    DC, 22
Carter, Ash, 143
Castro, Fidel, 152
Chalmette National Cemetery,
    25
Champion, Mary, *121*
Chaumont sur Haute Marne, 49
chemical warfare, 133
chlorine gas, 133
chocolate bars, 48, 111
citizen soldiers, 117, 118
Civil War (1861–1865), 2, 17, 21,
    23, 28, 33
Clarke, Charles, 31
coalition forces, 155, 156
Cochran, Margaret. *See* Corbin,
    Margaret Cochran
codes, military staff identifica-
    tion, 124
Cold War, 186
Columbus Dispatch, 77
Company D, 23rd Tank Battal-
    ion, 103
Confederate army, 21, 23, *33*
Continental army, 12
Cooper, Casey, *169*, 176
Corbin, John, 9–10
Corbin, Margaret Cochran,
    5–15, *9*, *13*

background, 7–9
as camp follower, 6–7, 9–10
as a cannoneer, 10, 11–12
DAR commemorative coin, 7
marriage to John Corbin, 9
pension received by, 14
personality of, 14–15
as prisoner of war, 12, 14
search for gravesite of, 5–6
Counts, Julie, 122
couriers, use of, 47
Cramer, Myron C., 64
Criminal Investigations Division (CID). See US Army Criminal Investigations Command

Daughters of the American Revolution (DAR), 5–6
Davis, Kenneth E., 135
D-day, 105
Direct Ground Combat Definition and Assignment Rule (1994), 141–142
discrimination, in the military, 28, 43, 75
Douglass, Ruby Jane, 68
Dunham, Mr. (school principal), 148
Dunwoody, Ann, x

Earley, Charity Adams, 72–86, 81, 85
background, 73–74
call to military service, 75–77
overseas assignments, 72–73, 79–84
postservice life, 85
segregation encountered by, 77–79
Efferson, Edith L., 113
8th Indiana Volunteer Infantry, 33–34
Emancipation Proclamation, 33
European Theater of Operations (ETO) mail service, 73, 80
Evening Star (Washington, DC), 39
Executive Order 9066, 90
Executive Order 9163, 77

Faith, Donald, 60
Faulkner, Deborah, 177
55th Materiel Management Center, 121
First Company of the Pennsylvania Artillery, 9
First Marine Expeditionary Force, 136
fitness test requirements, army, 127
Fort Bigham Massacre, 8–9
Fort Cummings, New Mexico, 35–36
Fort Des Moines, Iowa, 69, 77
Fort McClellan, Alabama, 100
Fort Washington, attack on, 11
447th Military Police Company, 149
Freedom Flotilla, 152

Garver, Paul, 148
Gender Integration Study (US Army), 143
Green Zone (Baghdad), 155

Hallaren, Mary Agnes, *112*
Harris, Diane, 151
Hawai'i, 88, 91
Hello Girls, *39*–40, *40*, 47–51, *50*,
    54, 57
    See also Banker, Grace
Hershey Chocolate Company,
    111
Hester, Leigh Ann, 168–178, *171*
    background, 170, 172
    deployments to Middle East,
        173–177
    medal recognition received
        by, 168–170
    as military police officer,
        172–177
    postservice life, 177–178
    See also Raven 42
Hobby, Oveta Culp, *42*, 58–71,
    60, 61, 67, 70
    background, 60, 62–63
    call to military service,
        41–42, 63–64
    as director of WAAC, 42,
        58–59, 64–69
    postservice life, *69*–71
    preservice employment, *63*
Hobby, William, 60, *63*
Hoisington, Bob, 103–104, 106
Hoisington, Elizabeth Paschel,
    101, 103–114, *110, 112, 113, 114*
    background, 104, 106
    call to military service, 104–
        105, 107–108
    death and burial, 113–114
    deployment to Europe,
        108–109

    medals received by, 109
    postservice life, 113
    promotions received by, 101,
        110, 113
    search for brother in Europe,
        103–104
    as WAC director, 110–113
Honolulu Star-Bulletin, 89
Hostetler, Mary A., 144–157, *146*,
    150, 157
    background, 147–148
    call to military service, 146
    as citizen soldier, 149–152,
        156
    as criminal investigator, 142,
        152–154
    postservice life, 156–157
    retirement from military life,
        144–146, 156
    as a state police officer, 150
    tour in Iraq, 154–156
Hussein, Saddam, 155, 173

internment camps, Japanese
    American, 90
invasion of Normandy. *See*
    D-day

Jackson, Francis, *121*
Japanese Americans, 90
Jefferson Barracks, 27
Jodl, Alfred, 83
Johnson, Melina, *121*
Johnson, Rita, 182
Jones, Kendra, *121*
Jump School. *See* Basic Airborne
    School

K rations, 108, 111
Kimball, Allen R., 109, *110*
Korean War (1950–1953), 100
Kotulich, Deborah L., 142, 179–
 190, *185*, *188*, *189*
 background, 181–183
 at the Berlin Wall, 184–185
 as citizen soldier, 187
 deployments, 183–186,
  187–189
 as logistics officer, 185–187
Kutch, Janice, 182

Laddie (dog), 116, *116*
Lavine, Abraham L., 51
Lee, John C. H., *81*
Lincoln, Abraham, 21, *23*, 33
Lincoln, Stephanie, 142, 158–
 167, *162*, *165*, *166*
 background, 160
 at boot camp, 161–164
 as citizen soldier, 160–161, 167
 as executive officer and drill
  instructor, 166–167
 as marksman, 158–159
 at Officer Candidate School,
  165–166
 postservice life, 167
Lister bags, 108
Logan, Paul, 111
Long, Greg, 152
Loyalists, 12

M1 tank simulation training,
 179–180
M151A1 army jeep, *150*
Magaw, Robert, 11

mail delivery, during World
 War II, 80–81
Marshall, George C., 42, *59*, 61,
 65
Martin, Gloria, *121*
McCoskrie, Frank U. "Colonel
 Mac," 79
McGuire, Colleen, 134
medical examinations, 3, 29–30
Merriam, Henry, 29
Mike, Jason, 169, *169*, 177
Military Police Corps, 151
military police officers (MPs),
 132, 149, 151–152
Mizell, Rhonda, *121*
Mogadishu, Somalia, 136
Molly Pitcher. *See* Corbin, Mar-
 garet Cochran
Myer, Albert J., 47

Naval Consolidated Brig, 134
Nein, Timothy, 169–170, *169*,
 176, 177
New York Times, 2, 143
9/11 attacks, 173
988th Military Police Company,
 151
North, the. *See* Union army

O'ahu, Hawai'i, 87–91
Ohio State Highway Patrol, 150,
 151
Old Capitol Prison, Washington, DC. *See* Carroll Prison,
 Washington, DC
143rd Expeditionary Sustainment Command (ESC), 189

153rd New York State Volunteers, 19–22, 24
Operation Desert Shield and Desert Storm, 101–102
Operation Enduring Freedom, 173
Operation Iraqi Freedom, 173
Operation Joint Endeavor, 121

Pallas Athene, 58, 68, 107
Panetta, Jimmy, 144–145
Parachutist Badge (Jump Wings), 182
Patriots, 12
Pearl Harbor attack, 87–90
pensions, military, 7, 14, 36–37
Pentagram (newspaper), 127
Pershing, John "Black Jack," 39, 51, 145
Personal Justice Denied, 90
Pewitt, Patricia C., 113
Pinkerton Detective Agency, 145
Powers, C. M., 29
Powers, Cheryl, 121
prisoners of war, 53, 84, 141
Public Law 554, 41

Quartermaster Corps. *See* US Army Quartermaster Corps
Quarters 54, 78

rank restrictions, on women, 100, 101
rappelling, Australian, 129, 131
rations, food, 111

Raven 42 (military police unit), 142, 175–176
Ray, Lana, 121
Ready, Captain, 113
Reamy, Nancy, 121
Rebels, 33
Red River Campaign, 24
relocation centers, Japanese American, 90
Republican Palace, 154, 155
Reserve Army Corps. *See* US Army Reserve
reservists, 100, 119
Roberts, Sharon, 121
Rogers, Edith Nourse, 59, 61
Roosevelt, Eleanor, 61, 61
Roosevelt, Franklin, 41, 77, 90
Royster, Diana, 121

Salman Pak, 175
Searles, Towanda, 121
second lieutenants, 184
segregation, 75, 78, 79, 95
Sheppard, Karen, 121
Sheridan, Philip, 34
Signal Corps. *See* US Army Signal Corps
Silver Star Medal, 171, 172
617th Military Police Company, 174
6888th Central Postal Directory Battalion, 43, 73, 74, 79–83, 82, 85
slavery, 23, 33
Smithen, Bernadette, 121
Somalia, 136–137
South, the, 33

SS *Matsonia*, 94
St. *Paul Pioneer*, 3
Stoabs, Rhynell M., *113*
Sun magazine, 112
Surles, Alexander Day, 41, 62, 64
Swieczkowski, LeAnn, 126–139, *138*
  as army public affairs specialist in Somalia, 135–138
  at basic training camp, 128–129, 131–132
  enlistment of, 128
  military family background, 127–128
  as military police officer, 132–135
  physical fitness of, 126–127
  postservice life, 138–139

telephone operators. *See* Hello GIrls
telephones, use of
  code word usage in, 52
  military regulations regarding, 49–50, 51–52
  in World War I, 47, 51
3rd Platoon Women's Army Auxiliary Corps (WAAC), *78*
Thirteenth Amendment (US Constitution), 23
38th United States Infantry, Company A, 31, *36*
375th CID Detachment, 154
Time magazine, 65
Truman, Harry S., 97, 99
200th Military Police Command, 146

Ulio, James Alexander, *60*
Union army, 21, 23, 33
United Service Organization (USO), 93
United States Disciplinary Barracks (USDB), 132–135
US Army Criminal Investigations Command, 145, 152–153
US Army Gender Integration Study, 143
US Army Quartermaster Corps, 119
US Army Reserve (USAR), 102, 118, 119
US Army Signal Corps, 44, 47
US Army Women's Museum, 170, 178
US Field Ration D, 111
US Military Academy. *See* West Point Military Academy
US Regular Army, 27, 28, 99, 117
US War Department, 22, 41–42, 57, 61, 62, 92
USS *Arizona*, 89

Velazquez, Loreta Janeta, 2
Victory in Europe Day (V-E Day), 82, 83
Victory over Japan Day (V-J Day), 97
Vines, John R., 168, *169*, 170

WAAC. *See* Women's Army Auxiliary Corps
WAAC Officer Candidate School, Fort Des Moines, Iowa, *78*, 108

WAC. *See* Women's Army
Corps
WAC Center and School, 100
Wakeman, Emily Celestia, 18
Wakeman, Sarah Rosetta
"Lyons," 3, 16–25, *19*
background, 17–19
as Civil War soldier, 19–25
gravesite of, *24, 25*
Walls, Nina, *121*
War Department. *See* US War
Department
War on Terror, 173
Warrant Officer Candidate
School, Fort Rucker, 153
Washington, DC, 22
Washington, George, 8, 184
Welch, Shannon, *121*
West Point Military Academy,
101, 184
Wheeler Field, 88, 91
Williams, Cathay, 3, 26–37, *30, 32*
background, 32
as Buffalo Soldier, 34–36
conscription of, 32–34
denial of military pension
for, 36–37
enlistment of, 27–31
health issues, *35, 36*
postservice life, 36–37
Wilson, Mary Roberts, 172
Wittenmyer, Annie, 16
women, in the military
compensation for, 69
discrimination against, 43
in early America, 1–4
in Military Police Corps, 151

regulations regarding assignments of, 141–142
role of, 124
Women's Armed Services Integration Act (1948), 43, 99–100
Women's Army Auxiliary
Corps (WAAC)
compensation for, 69
early criticisms of, 59
establishment of, 41, 77
first African American officer
in, 79
first director of, 42, 64
Officer Candidate School, *78,*
108
officer recruitment for, 65,
66, 69, 77
origins of, 61, 62
professional image of, 68
song honoring, 68
success of, 42–43
symbol of, 68–69
transition to Women's Army
Corps, 41, 77, 107
uniforms, 66–68
See also Women's Army Corps
Women's Army Corps (WAC)
army firsts achieved by members of, 101–102, 118–119
directors of. *see* Hobby,
Oveta Culp; Hoisington,
Elizabeth Paschel
disestablishment of, 117
integration into armed
forces, 43
in Korean and Vietnam
Wars, 100

number of women in and
jobs held by, 42, 70–71, 112
prejudice in, 84
recruitment in Hawaiʻi, 93
restrictions imposed on,
99–100, 101
6888th Battalion of, 80
song honoring Hawaiʻian,
97–98
symbol of, 113
training facility for, 100
transition from Women's
Army Auxiliary Corps, 41,
77, 107
in World War II, 108–110
See also Women's Army Auxiliary Corps
World Powerlifting Federation
competition, 126–127

World War I, 39
World War II, 41, 75, 83, 97, 105,
111

Yang, Joe, 94
Yang, Margaret KC, 43, 87–98,
92, 94, 96
background, 91–92
defiance of Southern segregation by, 95
enlistment of, 93–94
Pearl Harbor attack and,
87–91
postservice life, 97
stateside assignments,
94–95
Yarbrough, John, 135

Zouave uniforms, 34–35